Golden Years

of

Birmingham

Part of the

Memories

series

The Publishers would like to thank the following companies for
supporting the production of this book

Armac Manufacturing Brass Founders

Aston & Fincher Limited

Barker Bretell

Birmingham College of Food, Tourism & Creative Studies

BID - Services for Deaf People

Boxmag-Rapid Limited

Buncher & Haseler Limited

Burcas Limited

Chesterton

Crofts & Assinder Limited

Druckers Patisserie

Dunnetts (Birmingham) Limited

Edgbaston High School for Girls

Flight's Coach Travel Limited

Gabriel & Company Limited

AJ Gilbert

Hiatts

George Lane & Sons Limited

Lee Longland & Company Limited

Loves plc

Henry Mills Limited

Parker-Hale Limited

William Sapcote & Sons Limited

Shakespeares Solicitors

AB Taylor Funeral Services Limited

Whites Removals & Transport Limited

First published in Great Britain by True North Books Limited
Units 3 - 5 Heathfield Industrial Park
Elland West Yorkshire
HX5 9AE
Tel. 01422 377977
© Copyright: True North Books Limited 1999

ISBN 1 900463 04 0

Text, design and origination by True North Books Limited
Printed and bound by The Amadeus Press Limited

Memories are made of this

Memories. We all have them; some good, some bad, but our memories of the area we grew up in are usually tucked away in a very special place in our minds. The best are usually connected with our childhood and youth, when we longed to be grown up and paid no attention to adults who told us to enjoy being young, as these were the best years of our lives. We look back now and realise that they were right.

So many memories - perhaps of the war and rationing, perhaps of parades, celebrations, Royal visits and sporting triumphs. And so many changes; one-way traffic systems and pedestrianisation. New trends in shopping that led to the very first self-service stores being opened.

Through the bad times and the good, however, Birmingham not only survived but prospered. We have only to look at the city as it is today, with its finest buildings restored to their full glory, and now complemented by up-to-the-minute facilities, to see what progress has been realised and what achievements have been made over the last 50 years. Birmingham has a history to be proud of - but more importantly, a great future to look forward to, into the new millennium and beyond.

Contents

Around the city centre

The broad, straight vista of Corporation Street, lined by some fine buildings, suggests that Joseph Chamberlain's nineteenth century scheme of turning it into a 'Parisian boulevard' was not entirely fanciful. This 1951 photograph looks up Corporation Street towards its intersection with Bull Street and it was here, in 1885, that Chamberlain persuaded David Lewis to open a new shop to grace his boulevard. A fanfare of trumpets announced the opening of Lewis's, a store which remained central to Birmingham's shopping culture until its closure in 1991. Not that some of the buildings lower down would have done

anything to offend Chamberlain's taste in terms of architecture that promoted civic pride. The elegant facade of the Cobden Hotel, to the left, is a case in point, with the symmetry of its pillars, balconies and arches. Further up Corporation Street, again to the left, the solid white building was to become a new £6 million Rackham's Store in 1960. It's a busy time in the picture, and these 1951 shoppers would find many of the shop frontages on Corporation Street much the same today, albeit with different names above them. However, that wonderful old horse-drawn delivery wagon would cause a bit of a stir now.

There seems to be plenty of appetite for shopping on Corporation Street in this scene from around 1946. The clothing of that time is very much in evidence, and the two soldiers gazing into the window of Perry & Co appear to be in American uniform. The main problem about shopping at this time was rationing. The need for coupons, and the rather dreary and limited range of 'utility' goods available, meant that shopping was often a search for that bit extra from 'under the counter'. The 'black market' flourished, but in this respect the well-paid American soldiers seemed to be able to afford even really expensive items such as cigarettes and nylons. No wonder they were popular with the local girls, but the lament of the local males was that the Yanks were,

A glance at the 1930s

WHAT'S ON?
In this heyday of the cinema, horrified audiences were left gasping at the sight of Fay Wray in the clutches of the giant ape in the film 'King Kong', released in 1933. Very different but just as gripping was the gutsy 1939 American Civil War romance 'Gone with the Wind'. Gable's parting words, 'Frankly, my dear, I don't give a damn' went down in history.

GETTING AROUND
At the beginning of the decade many believed that the airship was the transport of the future. The R101 airship, however, loaded with thousands of cubic metres of hydrogen, crashed in France on its maiden flight in 1930. Forty-eight passengers and crew lost their lives. In 1937 the Hindenburg burst into flames - the entire disaster caught on camera and described by a distraught reporter. The days of the airship were numbered.

SPORTING CHANCE
The black American Jesse Owens won a brilliant four world records in the 1936 Olympic Games in Berlin, thumbing the nose to Adolph Hitler's dreams of Aryan superiority. In a petty display Hitler walked out of the stadium and 'took his bat home'; later he refused to have his photograph taken with the victorious Owens.

'overpaid, over-sexed and over here'. Further up Corporation Street, the fine facade of the Cobden Hotel is visible. Such grand establishments were built to cater for the great age of rail travel, when businessmen almost always travelled by train and stayed overnight. The growth of mass private transport has radically altered travel patterns, and the Cobden is just one of many old hotels that no longer serve the purpose for which they were built.

Above: The two trams bearing down Corporation Street seem to be challenging the opposing traffic to get out of the way, including the brewery wagon in the foreground. The traffic on view gives this the appearance of being a 1940s shot, in which case the trams would not dominate Corporation Street for much longer. Cyclists and motor-cyclists would not miss the perilous encounters they sometimes had with wet and greasy tramlines, but many people regretted that, after 1953, these fine old vehicles no longer rattled and swayed around the streets. Another casualty was to be the 'Evening Despatch', advertised on the front of the tram and on the side of the van. This merged with the 'Evening Mail' in the early 1960s. Corporation Street was named after the corporation, or council, which ordered its construction in 1878. It bore all the hallmarks of Joseph Chamberlain's grandiose vision - a radical programme of slum clearance to create a wide boulevard on the Parisian model. Such schemes did not come easily, and it was not until 1903 that the road linking New Street and Aston Street was completed. Change is a continual process. C&A would develop the building on the right into a new structure, clad in Portland stone, around 1956.

It's the fashions of the forties to the fore, particularly the splendid display of ladies' hats in the foreground to the right. This shot of the bottom end of New Street dates from around 1945. A soldier crosses the street quite close to the camera, and it may be an army lorry that rumbles up the street in the distance. Although the obstruction in the middle might be assumed to be connected with bomb damage, the hydrant at the front makes it more probable that it related to emergency water supplies for fire-fighting during air raids. Nevertheless, the picture does show a few scars that might have been the result of bombing, particularly on the left. In spite of the German bombers' main targets being Birmingham's engineering and aircraft factories, the city centre was heavily hit as well. The Market Hall had been burned out in August 1940, and in the October of that year the Council House, the Town Hall and the Art Gallery were all damaged. Fortunately these days were over by the time of the photograph, which seems to draw the eye to the tall Times Furniture building in the background. Today the Rotunda would probably be catching the eye.

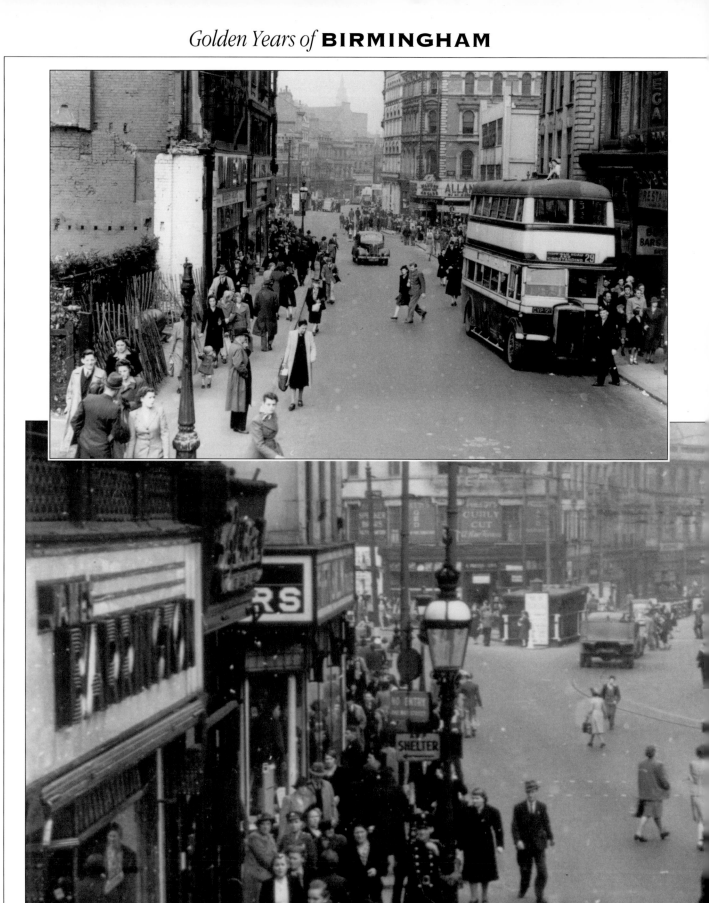

Left: High Street is possibly the oldest street in Birmingham, part of the old London Road, its name being a shortened version of the King's High Street. In this shot of 1946, however, it is looking distinctly battered. There is evidence of severe bomb damage to the left, including a gas lamp which appears to have had its top blown off. These may have been casualties of the first air raid on the city centre, on the night of August 25th 1940, when the nearby Market Hall was burned out and 25 people were killed. The grimness of the time may have been reflected in a rather limited menu at the Bodega Restaurant to the right. Nevertheless the name 'Bodega' has a rather racy feel about it, a reminder that people were still able to enjoy themselves. 1946 may have meant austerity, but it also meant 'jitterbugging' and the joyous shouting of, 'Hey-bob-a-reebob!' to the sound of jazz. Next to the damaged wall is a sign which proclaims, '5000 Coats To Choose From'. Perhaps this was a pre-war boast. River Island and Boots would now be found on the immediate left, with Marks & Spencer where the ladies are leaning out of the window, above the bus.

Below: The camera has been moved a little further down High Street for this second 1946 photograph, and the turn of one or two heads suggests that the photographer's activities have not gone unobserved. It was not as easy in 1946 to take a quick snap as it is now! The uniforms visible on the pavement to the left, along with the ARP (Air Raid Precaution) Shelter sign, show that the war had not long ended. A modern view would show Dorothy Perkins in place of Allans, and the Gas Showrooms further down High Street. The Argos Superstore would fill a good deal of the background. However, then as now, High Street belonged to the heartland of shopping country. For 1990s 'shopping centre' read 1940s 'arcade'. Wilson's Arcade appeared on the previous photograph [No 14], and in this one people are invited to, 'Wander Round The Arcade', at Allans. The Beehive, to the rear, proudly boasts of its Preedy's Curly Cut Tobacco, along with the rather mysterious Preedy's QED. To go back further, in 1882 Birmingham had so many arcades that the 'Mail' dubbed it an 'Arcadian town'. The ancient Greeks regarded Arcadia as a place of bliss. Do you belong to the group of people who believe that a shopping centre represents just that?

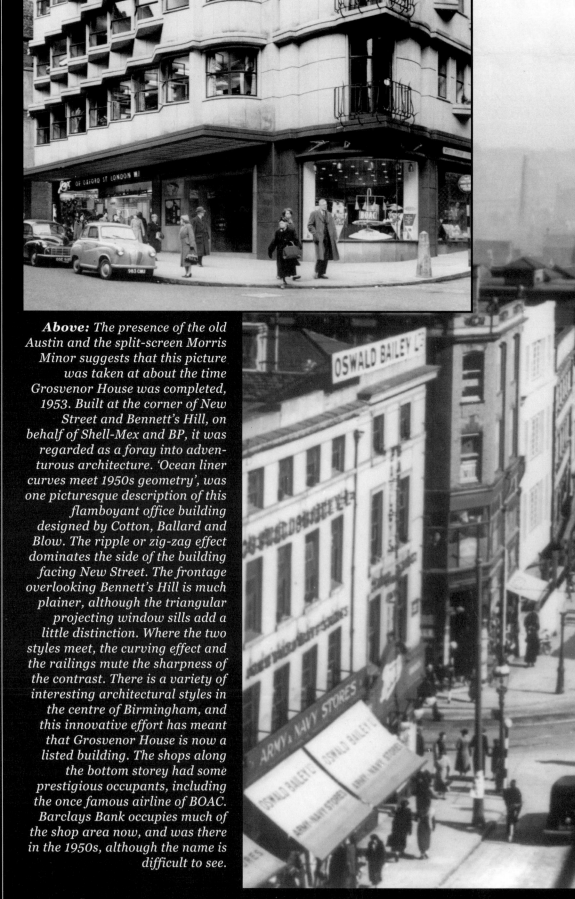

Above: *The presence of the old Austin and the split-screen Morris Minor suggests that this picture was taken at about the time Grosvenor House was completed, 1953. Built at the corner of New Street and Bennett's Hill, on behalf of Shell-Mex and BP, it was regarded as a foray into adventurous architecture. 'Ocean liner curves meet 1950s geometry', was one picturesque description of this flamboyant office building designed by Cotton, Ballard and Blow. The ripple or zig-zag effect dominates the side of the building facing New Street. The frontage overlooking Bennett's Hill is much plainer, although the triangular projecting window sills add a little distinction. Where the two styles meet, the curving effect and the railings mute the sharpness of the contrast. There is a variety of interesting architectural styles in the centre of Birmingham, and this innovative effort has meant that Grosvenor House is now a listed building. The shops along the bottom storey had some prestigious occupants, including the once famous airline of BOAC. Barclays Bank occupies much of the shop area now, and was there in the 1950s, although the name is difficult to see.*

St Martin's Church towers above the Bull Ring in this evocative photograph of 1937. It is the only feature in the foreground that would appear in a shot taken from the same angle today. The tramlines are nostalgic enough; even the bank of telephone boxes now have a quaint appearance; but it is the area itself, the Bull Ring, that conjures up the image of a rich historical tradition that has now vanished. The Bull Ring has always been at the heart of Birmingham's commercial life. In 1835 the Market Hall was opened, a huge building containing space for 600 stalls. A fish market followed in 1869, and a covered vegetable market was completed in Jamaica Row in 1884. The Bull Ring was also the site of two medieval fairs - the June or Pleasure Fair, and the Michaelmas or Onion Fair. The latter, in particular, was a noisy six day carnival, involving theatrical booths, menageries and swing boats. Ultimately, this became too much for Victorian ideas of 'respectability', and the fairs were banished from the town altogether in 1875. Nevertheless street traders, barrow boys, 'quack' doctors, soap-box orators and 'doomsday' preachers kept the Bull Ring as a centre for bargains and entertainment right up to World War II.

You can almost hear the piercing screams of the girls, whilst the more serious expressions on the faces of the young men suggest that driving dodgems really is a 'macho' male business. The clothes and hairstyles suggest the late 1950s, and the scene is probably Pat Collins' Fair, at Old Pleck. The magical attraction of fairs, that medley of sounds, movement and colour, has remained much the same through the ages. To visit Mander's Menagerie, or the 'Roil Famely Waxworks', was as much a thrill for nineteenth century visitors to the Onion Fair, at the Bull Ring, as are the waltzers and dodgems for the present generation. In fact the noise and boisterousness was too much for the 'sober and quiet people' of Birmingham, and the entertainments were evicted from the Bull Ring in 1875, to settle at Old Pleck. And what youngster can resist the fun of the fair, wherever it may be? Even the not so young will remember how the pulse quickened at the sound of the music and the sight of the bright lights against the night sky. Who can ever forget the strut of the fairground youths across the heaving speedway boards or that first sweet taste of candy floss?

At leisure

Is he wondering whether to spend his last tanner on the punchball, or has he already put the coin in the slot and nothing has happened? Perhaps he's just wondering how on earth he is going to reach it? This is a rare study in concentration amidst the noise and bustle of the fair in July 1953. The scene is Pat Collins' Fair at the Old Pleck, near Aston Church, which remained on that site until the Aston Expressway was driven through in the 1960s. The magnetic attraction of fairs goes back a long way. Medieval fairs had a trading focus, such as Birmingham's Horse and Onion Fairs, but they were always accompanied by a good deal of entertainment. Sideshows, menageries, sellers of tawdry souvenirs and purveyors of food and drink all provided the real 'fun of the fair'. This did not meet the approval of everyone. By 1781 William Hutton was describing the six day Onion Fair as simply an excuse for 'riot, drunkenness and mischief'. Perhaps not a lot has changed over the course of two centuries or more! It took a while for the authorities to heed such complaints, but in 1875 the enter-tainment trappings of the Onion Fair were banned from the town altogether - to end up where the boy is gazing at the punchball in 1953.

Golden Years of BIRMINGHAM

A glance at the 1930s

HOT OFF THE PRESS
The years of the 1930s saw Adolf Hitler's sickening anti-Jewish campaign echoed in the streets of Britain. On 19th October 1936 Oswald Mosley's 7,000-strong British Union of Fascists clashed head on with thousands of Jews and Communists in London, resulting in 80 people being injured in the ensuing battle. Mosley and his 'blackshirts' later rampaged through the streets beating up Jews and smashing the windows of their businesses.

THE WORLD AT LARGE
In India, Gandhi's peaceful protests against British rule were gathering momentum. The Salt Laws were a great bone of contention: forced to buy salt from the British government, thousands of protestors marched to the salt works, intending to take it over in the name of the Indian people. Policemen and guards attacked the marchers, but not one of them fought back. Gandhi, who earned for himself the name 'Mahatma' - Great Soul - was assassinated in 1948.

ROYAL WATCH
The talking point of the early 1930s was the affair of the Prince of Wales, who later became King Edward VIII, and American divorcee Wallis Simpson. Faced with a choice, Edward gave up his throne for 'the woman I love' and spent the remainder of his life in exile. Many supported him, though they might not have been as keen to do so if they had been aware of his Nazi sympathies, kept strictly under wraps at the time.

It's the claret and blue shirts on the attack, and it looks as if the forwards are claiming at least a corner in this evocative shot of Aston Villa playing Arsenal, at Villa Park, in 1952. Aston Villa have always been one of the great names of English football, even during their brief sojourns in the lower divisions. Founded by young men of the Villa Cross Wesleyan Chapel in 1874, the club became a founder member of the Football League in 1888. In an

16

astonishing seven seasons between 1893 and 1900, they were Football League Champions five times, winning the double of League and FA Cup in 1897. There were plenty of great days to come, but perhaps Villa's proudest moment was lifting the European Cup in 1982. The photograph harks back to an age of football 'innocence' - no all-covered. all-seated football stadium in 1952, with pre-purchase of tickets absolutely necessary. You came along and paid at the turnstiles and, as the foreground shows, children could play around or just sit on the grass at the top of the banking. On the other hand, safety standards were not high. It seems incredible to think that on March 2nd 1946, 76,588 people crammed into this ground.

Wartime

> *'E' Day signalled the evacuation of thousands of children from high-risk areas*

It's quick march across the playground for these youngsters from a Birmingham school in the early stages of World War II. However, it was no day trip or 'residential learning experience' that they were embarking upon. It was much more serious than that. These were among the thousands of Birmingham schoolchildren who were evacuated to escape German bombing. Personal possessions have been packed into a variety of suitcases, bags and haversacks, but the theme that is common to them all is that of the gas mask box and the identity label - the unmistakable marks of evacuees. As war loomed ever closer in 1939, the greatest fear of the government and local authorities was that of massive civilian casualties from heavy bombing. Plans were carefully prepared for the evacuation of schoolchildren from the expected target areas, although the initial scheme for Birmingham included only the central areas and those containing munition works. Britain declared war on Germany on September 3rd 1939, but evacuation rehearsals had started as far back as July 20th 1939. A full-scale rehearsal took placed on August 28th, before special messengers to schools on August 31st brought the information that the evacuation was on - the real thing - the following day!

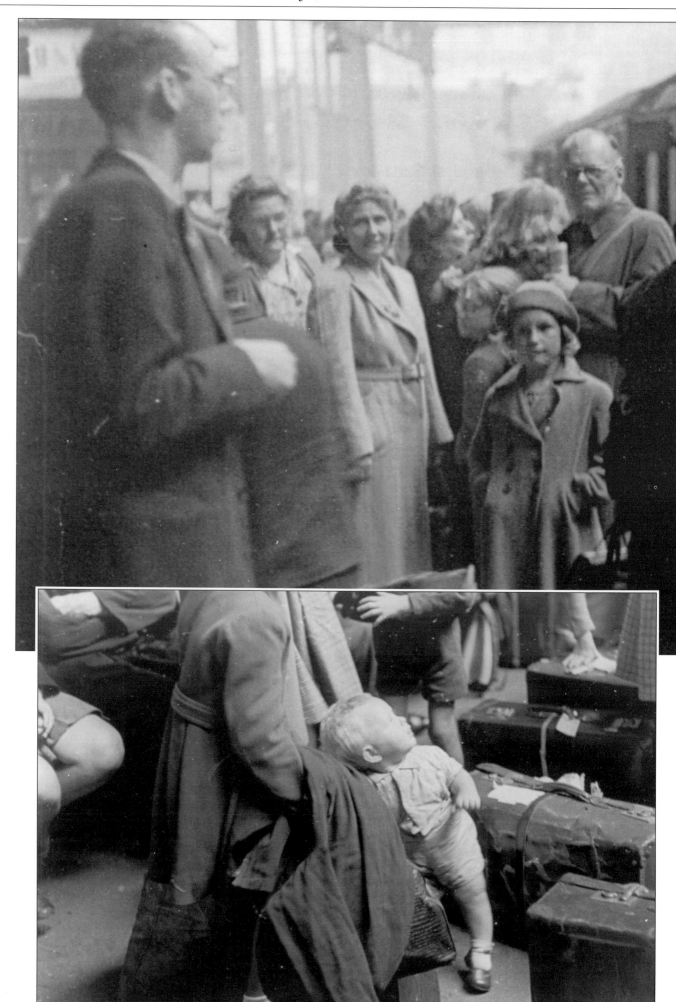

Left: The bewilderment on the face of this toddler seems to sum it all up. He seems to be looking skywards as if in anticipation of falling bombs, although he is more likely to be seeking reassurance in the face of some friendly adult. This photograph, and the one which follows it, show the scenes at Birmingham New Street station in September 1939 as evacuation got under way. Bewilderment was only one of many emotions that were felt by young and old alike during these uncertain days. Anxiety, strain, fear - these are some of the other emotions that are etched on the faces of people on the crowded platform. The evacuation which took place on September 1st 1939 was a voluntary one, and 240 buses had been reserved to transport some of the anticipated 73,000 children, although most were within marching distance of New Street, Snow Hill and Moor Street stations. Over 4000 teachers and helpers were to accompany the children. The authorities kept the destinations secret, even from parents. This was too much for some tearful mothers, who went to see their children off but promptly took them back home again!

Above: The trains that rolled away from the various platforms on September 1st 1939 could have been heading, literally, anywhere. They were probably not as full as antici-pated, for only one third of the expected 73,000 children had turned up for this voluntary venture. The children of Boulton Road Junior School, Handsworth, only went as far as Hagley, whereas the children of St Benedict's Road School, Small Heath, eventually found themselves in Ross-on-Wye. However, no child was to be more than 3½ hours journey away. Some of the children no doubt saw it all as a great adventure, but many of them must have felt as much distress as their parents. On September 2nd 1939 mothers with very small children were evacuated from Birmingham, numbering 12,377 in all, along with 406 expectant mothers and 20 handicapped adults. The declaration of war the following day brought a clamour for evacuation from the parents who had kept their children at home. The problem was, of course, that during the period known as the 'phoney war' there was scarcely any bombing anywhere, and parents began to bring their children home. However the bombing of Birmingham began in earnest in August 1940, and the evacuation process had to begin all over again.

This scene of destruction on Holliday Street in 1941 was one which the government had feared would be multiplied a millionfold across the country at the outbreak of World War II in September 1939. There was a comparative period of calm up to August 1940. Birmingham, however, with its engineering and munitions industries was high on the Luftwaffe's list, especially as 'shadow' factories making warplanes had been attached to the more traditional motor firms. The first bombs fell in August 1940. Although the prime aim of the German pilots was to hit factories and public utilities, inevitably homes suffered as well. The photograph shows a typical situation in which the attack was aimed at Barber Switchgear, but bombs have also totally cross-sectioned a neighbouring house. Raids of varying intensity continued until April 1943. Probably the heaviest took place when 350 German bombers pounded Birmingham for almost the whole of the night of November 19th 1940. One incident which may well still be etched on some people's memories took placed on October 29th 1940, when a bomb exploded in front of the screen of the Carlton Cinema, in Sparkhill, killing 19 people. Overall, 2,241 Birmingham people paid the ultimate price for being in the vanguard of the Home Front.

Birmingham were proud of Neville Chamberlain, happy to declare him their 'greatest living citizen'. Sadly, he did not avert a world catastrophe - only delayed it. He was an honest and decent man, but he was putty in the hands of a man with such ruthless cunning as Hitler. It was a short step from the accolade of 'Peacemaker' to the sneer of 'Appeaser'.

Top: There are some very serious discussions going on between these neighbours in Oldknow Road, Small Heath, in August 1940. The date was a significant one for it marked the month during which the first bomb fell in Birmingham, killing an unfortunate man in Erdington. The scene gives every indication in itself of being a bomb site, but it is more than likely that the clutter is the result of the construction of Anderson shelters in the garden. Possibly the men are discussing technical problems which have arisen, but there is no doubt that the womenfolk are exchanging news of a grave nature. August 1940 marked the end of the 'phoney war' as far as Birmingham was concerned, but at least it had allowed a breathing space for the construction of air raid shelters on streets and in school and factory yards. The alternative was to have your own 'luxury' accommodation in the shape of an Anderson shelter. These were dug deep into gardens, leaving a semi-circle of corrugated metal, reinforced by turf and sandbags, above ground. Each one had six bunks, and although they were stuffy and uncomfortable, there is no doubt that some people owed their lives to them.

Above: It is easy, with hindsight, to simply shake one's head in disbelief at the billing over the News Theatre and dismiss it as a triumph of hope over experience. In those anxious days of September 1938, however, how many people walked not just the High Street of Birmingham, but the streets of cities all over Britain, and fervently hoped that at least some part of this message was true? Chamberlain had desperately wanted to be the peacemaker, as proclaimed on the poster, and had returned from Munich clutching the little piece of paper which, to him, represented 'Peace for our time'. Neville Chamberlain, Prime Minister of the day, was Birmingham's favourite son. He represented that strong political link between Birmingham and the Chamberlain family which dated back to 'Radical Joe' Chamberlain and his 'gas and water socialism' of the 1870s. The people of

A glance at the 1940s

WHAT'S ON?
In wartime Britain few families were without a wireless set. It was the most popular form of entertainment, and programmes such as ITMA and Music While You Work provided the people with an escape from the harsh realities of bombing raids and ration books. In 1946 the BBC introduced the Light Programme, the Home Service and the Third Programme, which gave audiences a wider choice of listening.

GETTING AROUND
October 1948 saw the production of Britain's first new car designs since before the war. The Morris Minor was destined for fame as one of the most popular family cars, while the four-wheel-drive Land Rover answered the need for a British-made off-road vehicle.
The country was deeply in the red, however, because of overseas debts incurred during the war. The post-war export drive that followed meant that British drivers had a long wait for their own new car.

SPORTING CHANCE
American World Heavyweight Boxing Champion Joe Louis, who first took the title back in 1937, ruled the world of boxing during the 1940s, making a name for himself as unbeatable. Time after time he successfully defended his title against all comers, finally retiring in 1948 after fighting an amazing 25 title bouts throughout his boxing career. Louis died in 1981 at the age of 67.

'It's all over!' Young and old alike share in the joy of VE Day (Victory in Europe) at this street party on Heeley Road, Selly Oak, on May 8th 1945. The news was greeted by relief, but also a certain amount of reflection in Birmingham. By lunchtime of the great day, the city centre was thronged with happy crowds, and street vendors of rosettes and posies in patriotic colours were doing a roaring trade. By evening a crowd of around 30,000 had

squeezed itself into Victoria Square, and the immediate vicinity, to hear King George VI's broadcast over a relay system. Then it was time for dancing, singing and rejoicing until dawn. In the suburbs it was a case of street parties, bonfires and numerous burnings of effigies of Hitler. Nevertheless, the joy was tinged with a little sadness, as reflected in the large

attendances at the many church services held that day. The war was not over; Japan was fighting on. Prayers were no doubt offered up for the men of Birmingham still involved in the conflict, or for those about whom no news had been received for a long time. Some Birmingham households knew already of course, that their menfolk were never going to return at all.

Events & occasions

The days of shortages and rationing did not end in 1945. It was still a rather drab and austere post-war Britain until the 1950s, and so the people of Birmingham welcomed the touch of colour and pageantry that was occasioned by a royal visit. The scene is New Street Station, May 11th 1948. King George VI, accompanied by Queen Elizabeth, have just been greeted by the Mayor and Mayoress, Mr and Mrs J C Burman. Dense and cheering crowds lined the route of the three and a half mile car tour which preceded the arrival of the royal couple at the Town Hall. There the Mayor presented them with a silver wedding gift from Birmingham - a mahogany canteen of engraved silver forks and spoons. The King made a token return friendship gift of a newly minted one penny piece. After lunch the royal party proceeded to the British Industries Fair at Castle Bromwich. Both King George and Queen Elizabeth displayed much interest in the state of British industry, and the Queen ordered a pressure cooker from the Midland Metal Spinning Company. The drive to Stechford Station, for departure, was given another tumultuous reception, and it was estimated that over 300,000 people had greeted the royal couple that day.

Below: It's a fairly quiet time on New Street in May 1937, and from the raincoats draped over one or two arms it appears to be 'typical' May weather in England. However, the view from Marshall and Snelgrove, looking towards the High Street, demonstrates that something is definitely 'in the air'. The Coronation of George VI was the reason for the decorations, but the embellishment of the streets was only one aspect of preparing for the great day. The Mayor of Birmingham was granted a £15,000 increase in his allowance, and this was to cover decorations, fireworks, concerts and an illuminated tramcar to tour the city. The grant was also to fund the cost of providing 2s 6d (12 $\frac{1}{2}$ p) to all citizens over the age of 65, and not in receipt of public assistance; £1 to each child born on Coronation Day, May 12th; 1s 1d (6p) to all secondary school children;

and mugs and souvenir tins of chocolate to all elementary schoolchildren. It would be interesting to know how many mugs and chocolate tins still survive today - collectors' items surely. The private sector did its bit in that the Birmingham Municipal Bank offered to open accounts for all local children born between May 9th and May 15th, with a gift of 5 shillings (25p) as an initial deposit.

Bottom: This high-angled shot of Corporation Street on the eve of the 1937 Coronation shows two remarkable things - firstly the splendour of the decorations and secondly the volume of traffic. Certainly the number of cars pouring down Corporation Street seems surprising for a time that was well before the age of mass car ownership. However, the Esso sign would definitely be redundant now in a city centre of restricted vehicular access. The decorating of the central area of the city was the responsibility of the Chamber of Commerce, and the much admired decorated touring tram was illuminated at night by 1050 bulbs. Public events of this sort are a tremendous boost to trade, which is why the commercial world had been so aghast in 1936 at the pre-Coronation abdication of Edward VIII, and the prospect of cancelled orders. However, all was made right the following year, and Birmingham's four leading wholesalers were kept busy in supplying 1 $\frac{1}{2}$ million flags, 1 $\frac{1}{2}$ million yards of bunting, 1 $\frac{1}{2}$ million yards of ribbon and $\frac{1}{2}$ million balloons and caps. The Birmingham composer, Hubert B Parker, entered into the spirit of it all by sending a Coronation anthem to King George VI, for which he received a letter of thanks.

If Hubert B Parker found inspiration for his music in the Coronation of 1937, then the students at Birmingham's School of Art were given a unique opportunity to utilise their creative skills. It was decided that one aspect of the city centre decorations should concern heraldry, and the brief for the students was to create over 50 shields on which would be emblazoned the coats-of-arms of the families which had been prominently connected with Birmingham's history. The consultant was to be Mr S C Kaines Smith, Curator of the Birmingham Museum and Art Gallery. The photograph of Victoria Square in May 1937 shows some of these shields displayed on the Council House, to the left. The 11 metre high column in the foreground was another Coronation 'special effect'. It was surmounted by the gilded figure of St George on horseback, presenting the crown, and surrounded by four boxes of rhododendrons. The picture in itself holds great interest because Victoria Square has changed so radically. The whole block facing Queen Victoria's stony stare has now vanished, as has the statue of her royal consort, Albert. Perhaps the most famous feature of this block was one of the well-known Lyons 'corner' shops.

Above: It is little wonder that one of the most popular sightseeing destinations for people from all over the Midlands, in May 1937, was Birmingham city centre. Visitors flocked in to marvel at the street decorations which had been put up to mark the Coronation of George VI on May 12th 1937. Not many, however, will have enjoyed this elevated view of New Street proudly displaying its banners, which seem to stretch endlessly into the distance. A great deal of planning had gone into the creation of these banners and standards in order to make them a celebration of Britain, its Empire and the Dominions. The high standards along each side of New Street each bore a nationalistic emblem at the bottom - a rose, a shamrock, a thistle or a leek. The smaller banners, towards the middle, carried both British and Imperial devices. For example, in the foreground can clearly be seen the maple leaf of Canada to the left, and the kangaroo of Australia to the right. The next set of banners has the star of India on the left. Such emblems were very fitting for a city with such wide trading links across the Empire and Dominions.

Birmingham's coronation decorations were considered among the best in the country

Left: The Coronation decorations at ground level, as seen in this view of High Street, are as impressive as from the higher angle of the previous photograph. This is what visitors and residents alike will have seen, and there is little wonder that local people believed them to be the finest decorative display ever seen in Birmingham. Indeed one well-travelled man, and not a local, declared that they were the best in the country, outside London. The theme for High Street was purely a national one, with the tasselled banners swinging high in the air, and carrying the crosses of St George, St Andrew and St Patrick. Elsewhere can be seen the Welsh leek paired with the Irish shamrock, and the English rose paired with the Scottish thistle. The rather aggressive looking top section of the city's coat-of-arms also appears in sequence. What we cannot enjoy, of course, is the mass and profusion of colour which must have greeted the eye. Red, white and blue predominated, but there was also a good deal of green and gold to give what must have been a stunning effect. As for the congestion below, the policeman's face says it all.

Above: The lavish treatment endowed on the city centre streets was matched by imaginative schemes for public buildings. This photograph captures the edge of perhaps the city's most poignant building, the Hall of Memory, built as a fitting memorial to the dead of World War I. The area in front of it features some of the floodlights which illuminated it over a succession of nights during the Coronation period. Other buildings to receive this spectacular treatment included the Council House, the Town Hall, St Philip's Cathedral and St Martin's Church. Interesting colour schemes were experimented with. The Central Fire Station, for example, had its engine exits illuminated in a glowing red. Hence the citizens of Birmingham could wander by night and enjoy the spectacle of a floodlit Britannia, surrounded by mermaids, on the Town Hall. The lighting effects turned the garlands on the Corinthian columns to a glinting green and gold. The colours on the heraldic shields were given enhanced brilliance by the flood-lighting, particularly the ones on the Council House which showed the arms of the Lords of Birmingham from 1166 to 1824. The Hall of Memory was to be floodlit only once more before the dark days of World War II brought more additions to the Book of Memory.

A glance at the 1940s

HOT OFF THE PRESS

At the end of World War II in 1945 the Allies had their first sight of the unspeakable horrors of the Nazi extermination camps they had only heard of until then. In January, 4,000 emaciated prisoners more dead than alive were liberated by the Russians from Auschwitz in Poland, where three million people, most of them Jews, were murdered. The following year 23 prominent Nazis faced justice at Nuremberg; 12 of them were sentenced to death for crimes against humanity.

THE WORLD AT LARGE

The desert area of Alamogordo in New Mexico was the scene of the first atomic bomb detonation on July 16, 1945. With an explosive power equal to more than 15,000 tons of TNT, the flash could be seen 180 miles away. President Truman judged that the bomb could secure victory over Japan with far less loss of US lives than a conventional invasion, and on 6th August the first of the new weapons was dropped on Hiroshima. Around 80,000 people died.

ROYAL WATCH

By the end of World War II, the 19-year-old Princess Elizabeth and her distant cousin Lieutenant Philip Mountbatten RN were already in love. The King and Queen approved of Elizabeth's choice of husband, though they realised that she was rather young and had not mixed with many other young men. The couple's wedding on 20th November 1947 was a glittering occasion - the first royal pageantry since before the war.

One problem with the Coronation decorations, which is as apparent with the photograph of High Street as with this one of New Street, was that they tended to mask some of the fine architectural features of Birmingham's city centre buildings. However, no doubt this was amply compensated for by the colour which was brought to the streets. A Coronation is meant to be a unifying occasion, and this was the decorative theme -

many nations united under one flag and crown. The latter is a prominent feature repeated down the centre of New Street, the crowns being garlanded with paperchains. The long standards flanking the streets have a simplicity about them which contrasts with the richness of the banners, but each standard has either a national symbol at the bottom, or part of the city arms. The pair of banners in the foreground, on either side of the crown, carry the Bowes arms of the Queen and Wales (to the right) and the lion arms of Queen Elizabeth. The following pair of banners carry the rampant lion of Scotland and the triple lions of England. Banners representing the Empire and the Dominions follow on.

Above: Corporation Street as viewed from New Street in May 1937 shows some interesting features of the time. The One Way sign represents an early attempt to control traffic flows. There is also some attempt to protect pedestrians, but although the notice on the far right is uncompromising enough, we are well before the days of zebra crossings and little green men. Not long afterwards, however, as the decorations imply, all traffic was to be cleared from the streets to allow for the grand parade. This was the central event by which Birmingham celebrated the Coronation of George VI on May 12th 1937. The day was a rather cold one, but people were soon gathering three or four deep along the streets in the heart of the city. The tendency sometimes is for people to participate in such public occasions by means of their own floats, but this was a distinctly military parade including over 5,000 men and 250 nurses. It was headed by the band of the 1st Battalion of the Royal Scots, resplendent in gold and scarlet uniforms. The marchers assembled in Corporation Square, and such was the length of the procession that the vanguard had returned there before the last units set out!

Right: There is something about the precision and sound of a military parade that never fails to stir, even in these sophisticated days. How much more powerful the appeal of such a spectacle must have seemed in the 1930s, an age which lacked entertainment in the living room at the touch of a button. Each unit received its round of applause - the Royal Navy, the Seaforth Highlanders, the Territorial Army, the Auxiliary Air Force and other military units. Firemen, nurses and the St John's Ambulance Brigade had their place, as did the Officers' Training Corps of Birmingham University and cadets. However, the greatest applause and cheering was reserved for 150 veterans of the Second Boer War and 320 "Old Contemptibles" from World War I. However, May 12th 1937 was not entirely concerned with military preoccupations. Many people visited churches to listen to the Coronation ceremony relayed from Westminster Abbey. The St Martin's Guild of Church Bellringers was kept busy at a number of churches. Band concerts took place at 21 parks, with fireworks and flood-lighting in the evening. Street parties abounded in the suburbs, with fancy dress and entertainments. As a curious footnote, local hospitals dealt with many broken legs result-ing from old people taking part in street races!

The route of the grand military parade lay along Steelhouse Lane and Colmore Row into Victoria Square. Here the salute was taken by the Deputy Mayor whilst the band of the Royal Warwickshire Regiment played the units past. Other bands accompanied the parade with stirring martial music on the one and three quarter mile route of the procession, which was watched by around 250,000 people. After Victoria Square the marching columns moved through New Street and High Street 'en route' to Corporation Street. Both the photographs of New Street [this page] and High Street [previous page]

show busy scenes prior to Coronation Day, although all is in readiness in terms of the striking decorations. New Street in particular is thronged just outside the offices of the 'Birmingham Post and Mail', whilst further along the street the famous name of Pickfords may be seen on the delivery van. On the great day itself, however, the only 'traffic' along these streets was that of marching men. The crowds were confined behind crush barriers, and the white caped policeman on point duty in High Street was probably standing shoulder to shoulder with his colleagues in order to help keep the crowds back.

The magnificence that was Snow Hill station had not long to last when this picture was taken in 1966. The pillars and pediments that spoke so eloquently of a former age had bitten the dust within a few years. The shape of things to come, at least for a decade or two, looms up in the background - a building of stifling uniformity, and so typical of the 1960s. The original station at Snow Hill was opened in 1852 to serve the Birmingham to Wolverhampton and Birmingham to Oxford routes. As part of the station, the Great Western Hotel was completed in 1863. A complete reconstruction between 1906 and 1912 resulted in the building pictured, which was reckoned to be one of the finest examples of a main line Great Western Railways station. Not for nothing was GWR sometimes said to stand for 'God's Wonderful Railway'! Snow Hill enjoyed many years as a premier main line station, but in this respect its days were numbered with the electrification of the line between London Euston and New Street station, Birmingham, around 1960. This faster service led to an equally rapid diminishing of the role of Snow Hill, and the featured building was demolished in the 1970s.

On the move

Below: Platform 7, Snow Hill station, and the presence of destination boards on carriages, along with a plentiful supply of porters on the platform, seems to suggest pre-Beeching and the glorious age of steam. Snow Hill had its fair share of that glory, with main line Great Western expresses stopping there. The station was opened in 1852, and had the accompanying grandeur of the Great Western Hotel by 1863. Its rebuilding between 1906 and 1912 made the station a truly imposing edifice. However, it lost its status as a main line station in 1967 when express services were concentrated on New Street due to the recent electrification of the Euston - New Street - Wolverhampton line. The great days for Snow Hill were over but it pottered on, running a local service to Wolverhampton, until it was closed to passenger traffic in 1972. In the meantime the hotel came down in 1969; the concourse was demolished in 1970; followed by the entire station in 1977. Only the fine wrought iron gates that had led into the concourse were saved. The site was used as a car park for some years, but Snow Hill station now lives again, albeit on a modest scale.

Bottom: Considering that it is almost noon on a weekday in July 1955, Snow Hill station has an almost eerily quiet air about it. This uncharacteristic situation was not due to a sudden collapse in business, but to the fact that a national rail strike had reduced the service at Snow Hill to a 'skeleton' one. However, the sparsely populated booking hall gave the photographer the chance to capture some of the fine architectural features on display. On the reconstruction of Snow Hill station between 1906 and 1912 the booking hall, or concourse, was one of the interior features which gave the station its reputation as one of the finest on the Great Western network. The camera does not really do justice to the wonderful arch of metal and glass which roofed the concourse. Also, although some of the advertised brand names are still familiar enough, the existence of first and third class booking bays gives a certain 'period' feel to the picture. The demolition of the concourse took place in 1970, some seven years before the entire station met the same fate. So solidly had the concourse been built, that it almost brought the rest of the station down prematurely when it was demolished.

Both pages: At first sight it appears as if it is the motorbike that is the centre of attraction for the large crowd outside the Midland Bank, Erdington, on July 4th 1953 (facing page). There are even heads peering out of the upper windows of the bank. No doubt the owner was giving it a bit of rev, and clearly it was a well-travelled machine, looking at its baggage panniers and 'GB' plate. However, it would create more interest today as a vintage bike than it did then. It was only a side-show. What the crowd had really come to see was the departure of Birmingham's last tram, from Erdington terminus. The photograph below features the true star of the show, a fine old Birmingham tram about to make its last journey to the depot, and in so doing perform the 'swansong' for all the city's trams. The frontage of the Midland Bank, as featured in the previous picture, can be seen on the left-hand side of this one in a scene that speaks so much of the 1950s - from the gas lamp and the old Ford Popular to the glistening tramlines curving across the setts. A large crowd has gathered to give the last tram a rousing send off, and

no doubt a cheer was raised as that distinctive engine whine was heard, and car no 616 swayed and rattled its way along the lines and back home for the last time. Trams had first made their appearance on Birmingham's streets in May 1872, when they were pulled by horses. The Nechells horse trams began life in 1884 and steam trams had also begun to trundle around the streets by this time. All went electric after 1906, and although there was some experimentation with battery or accumulator trams, and a system that hauled trams by means of a cable set in the road, overhead wires were finally settled on. By 1928 the maximum tram route mileage was reached with the opening of the Stechford extension - 79.19 miles. The rise of the motor bus began to make inroads into the tram population in the 1930s, and it was in this decade that there was a gradual conversion to trolley-buses. The crowds at the Erdington terminus on July 4th 1953 were acknowledging the end of an era. Perhaps they were also demonstrating an old lesson in life - that we don't realise how much we value some things until we are about to lose them.

Bird's eye view

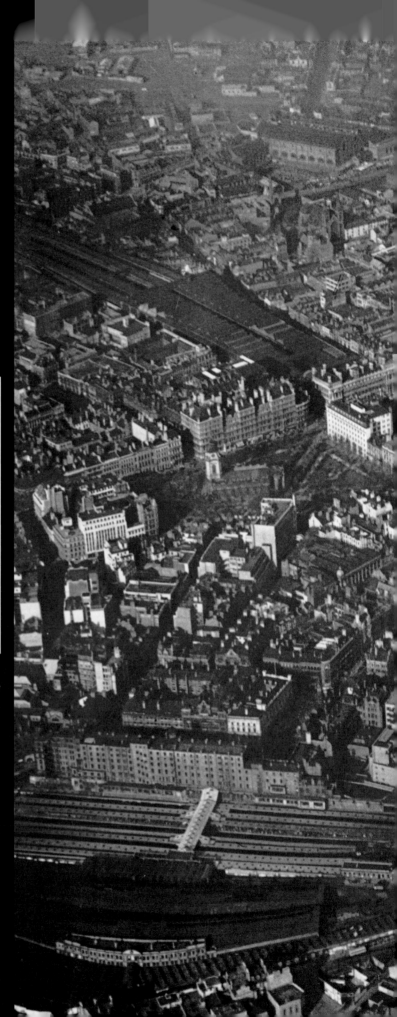

1948 saw a Birmingham prior to its excess of ring roads and islands

This 1948 aerial view of Birmingham encompasses a large part of the central area. We see a city centre of pre-development days, before the head-spinning proliferation of ring islands or circuses aimed at creating traffic flows which went around rather than through the heart of the city. Perhaps the best marker is Corporation Street, almost bisecting the photograph diagonally from bottom left towards top right. The Cobden Hotel, Lewis's, the Priory, the Old Square, the Victoria Law Courts and the Methodist Central Hall - these are the landmarks along it before it merges with Steelhouse Lane, close to where the Children's Hospital is today. The fire station is prominent - a little to the right. A left turn up Bull Street, in the lower reaches of Corporation Street, brings us out into the open area of St Philip's Cathedral, and just above that point is Snow Hill Station. Moving along the bottom part of the picture, from left to right, New Street and its station can be located. The famous old Bull Ring and St Martin's Church are visible towards bottom right. High Street and Moor Street stretch upwards from the Bull Ring, with Moor Street Station at lower right.

During World War II, enemy pilots who had Birmingham in their sights might well have seen a panorama such as this. Bomb damage was still much in evidence at the time of this aerial shot, 1948, although not from this height. A good reference point is St Philip's Cathedral, towards bottom centre. This was built in 1708 as the Parish Church, and it suffered severe fire damage from incendiary bombs in 1940. Luckily, the much valued Burne-Jones windows had already been removed to safety. Colmore Row runs diagonally along the bottom of the Cathedral, and following this upwards, to the left, brings us to Snow Hill Station. The building on view, a

combined Station Concourse and Great Western Hotel, had been constructed between 1906 and 1912. The Luftwaffe bears no responsibility for the destruction of this railway masterpiece. Planners were to accomplish this from 1969. After Snow Hill Station, Steelhouse Lane can be followed to its junction with Corporation Street at the very left edge. Corporation Street then may be traced roughly across the centre of the photograph, running slightly downwards from left to right, until it enters New Street. Landmarks along the right-hand side, moving upwards, are New Street Station, the Bull Ring and Moor Street Station.

The dome of the Hall of Memory, just left of centre, makes a good starting point for an examination of this 1948 aerial photograph. After World War I there were plans for an ambitious programme of civic building in this area, but finance was a problem. However the Hall of Memory, along with Baskerville House to the left, were two of the schemes which had borne fruit by the time of World War II. The Hall of Memory, an impressive memorial to those who had died in the 1914-18 conflict, was opened on July 4th 1925. Made of Cornish granite and Portland stone, over 30,000 people filed through on that first day. The rectangle in front of the Hall, which became Centenary Square in 1989, now has the Repertory Theatre, along with the International Convention Centre

A glance at the 1950s

WHAT'S ON?

Television hit Britain in a big way during the 1950s. Older readers will surely remember 'Double Your Money', 'Dixon of Dock Green' and 'Dragnet' (whose characters' names were changed 'to protect the innocent'). Commercial television was introduced on 22nd September 1955, and Gibbs SR toothpaste were drawn out of the hat to become the first advert to be shown. Many believed adverts to be vulgar, however, and audiences were far less than had been hoped for.

GETTING AROUND

The year 1959 saw the development of the world's first practical air-cushion vehicle - better known to us as the hovercraft. The earliest model was only able to travel at slow speeds over very calm water and was unable to carry more than three passengers. The faster and smoother alternative to the sea ferry quickly caught on, and by the 1970s a 170-ton car-carrying hovercraft service had been introduced across the English Channel.

SPORTING CHANCE

The four-minute mile had remained the record since 1945, and had become regarded as virtually unbreakable. On 6th May 1954, however, Oxford University student Roger Bannister literally ran away with the record, accomplishing the seemingly impossible in three minutes 59.4 seconds. Bannister collapsed at the end of his last amazing lap, even temporarily losing his vision. By the end of the day, however, he had recovered sufficiently to celebrate his achievement in a London night club!

and Symphony Hall, as its neighbours. Following Broad Street upwards, along the right flank of Centenary Square, brings us into the heart of Birmingham. Those with a keen eye will be able to locate the Town Hall, Victoria Square, the Council House and the Museum and Art Gallery. The streets which seem to converge on this area from the top of the picture are, from left to right, Great Charles Street, Edmund Street, Colmore Row, Waterloo Street and New Street.

Office blocks and administrative centres seem to dominate this aerial shot, which was probably taken in the early 1960s rebuilding phase. The best reference point is the tower of the Methodist Central Hall at top left of the picture. In front of the Methodist Hall the long stretch of Corporation Street runs across the photograph, intersecting with Newton Street. The Queen Elizabeth II Law Courts are now to be found just above this point. The Victoria Law Courts occupy much of the block between the Methodist Hall and Steelhouse Lane. To continue along Corporation Street to the right, flanking the huge central block, brings one into Old Square. The highway progressing from here to the top right-hand corner of the shot is now Priory Queensway. The empty site on the right of this would be developed first for Tesco, but is now an Argos superstore. Sweeping round the top edge of this bird's eye panorama we would now find James Watt Queensway, heading for Lancaster Circus. Some traffic is visible, but any comparable 1990s shot, taken at almost any time of the day, would see a greatly increased volume.

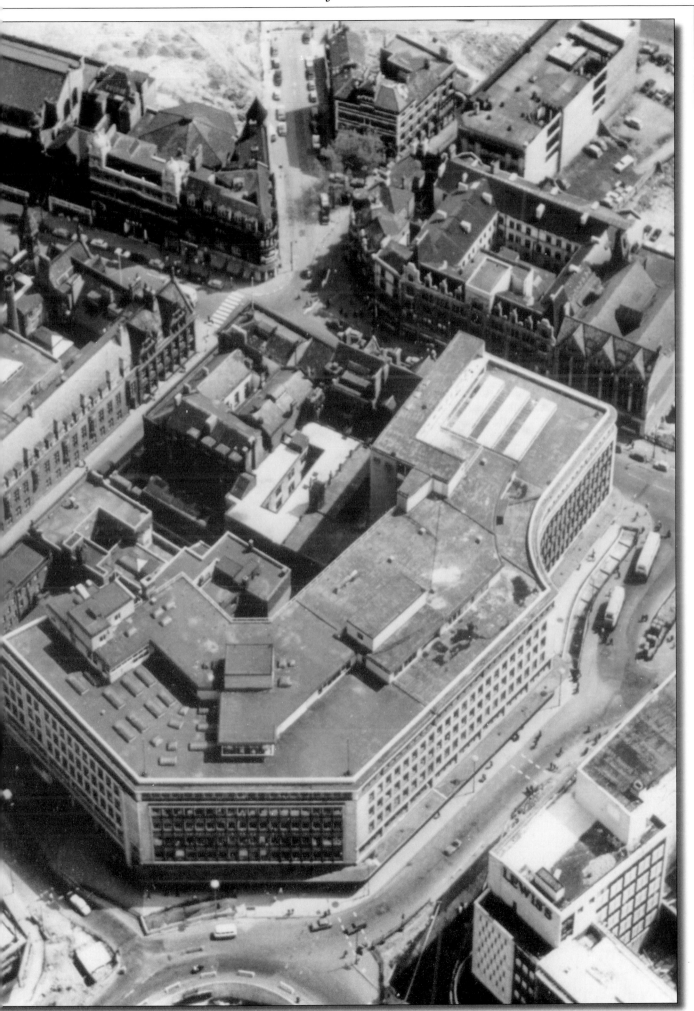

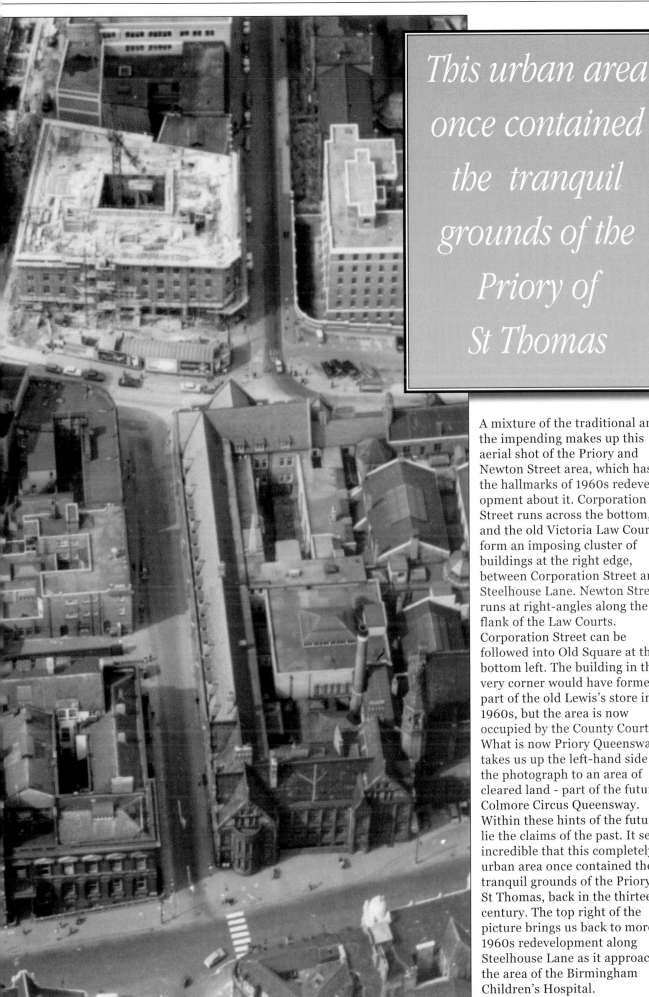

This urban area once contained the tranquil grounds of the Priory of St Thomas

A mixture of the traditional and the impending makes up this aerial shot of the Priory and Newton Street area, which has all the hallmarks of 1960s redevelopment about it. Corporation Street runs across the bottom, and the old Victoria Law Courts form an imposing cluster of buildings at the right edge, between Corporation Street and Steelhouse Lane. Newton Street runs at right-angles along the flank of the Law Courts. Corporation Street can be followed into Old Square at the bottom left. The building in the very corner would have formed part of the old Lewis's store in the 1960s, but the area is now occupied by the County Court. What is now Priory Queensway takes us up the left-hand side of the photograph to an area of cleared land - part of the future Colmore Circus Queensway. Within these hints of the future lie the claims of the past. It seems incredible that this completely urban area once contained the tranquil grounds of the Priory of St Thomas, back in the thirteenth century. The top right of the picture brings us back to more 1960s redevelopment along Steelhouse Lane as it approaches the area of the Birmingham Children's Hospital.

A glance at the 1950s

HOT OFF THE PRESS
The 1950s seemed to be the heyday of spies, and in 1951 the activities of Guy Burgess and Donald Maclean caused a sensation in the country. Both had occupied prominent positions in the Foreign Office, while Burgess had also been a member of MI-6. Recruited by the Russians while at Cambridge University in the 1930s, the traitors provided the Soviets with a huge amount of valuable information. They disappeared in 1951, surfacing in Moscow five years later.

THE WORLD AT LARGE
Plans to develop the economies of member states into one common market came to fruition on 1st January 1958, when the EEC came into operation. The original members were France, Belgium, Luxembourg, The Netherlands, Italy, and West Germany. The Community became highly successful, achieving increased trade and prosperity across Western Europe while at the same time alleviating fear of war which lingered on after the end of World War II. Britain became a member in 1973.

ROYAL WATCH
King George VI's health had been causing problems since 1948, when he developed thrombosis. In 1951 the King - always a heavy smoker - became ill again, and was eventually found to be suffering from lung cancer. His left lung was removed in September of 1951. In January 1952 he waved Princess Elizabeth and Prince Philip off on their tour of Africa; they were never to see him again. The King died on 5th February 1952.

We find ourselves right above the very heart of Birmingham city centre in an aerial shot which, from the appearance of many of the buildings, dates from the 1960s. The three more-or-less parallel streets moving upwards from the bottom of the photograph are, from left to right, Colmore Row, Edmund Street and Great Charles Street. The centre of the picture is occupied by the block of buildings making up the Museum and Art Gallery, along with

Council House. The classical shape of the Town Hall is clearly visible to the far left, with the old Reference Library and the Birmingham Midland Institute alongside it. Towards the top of the picture stands the landmark dome of the Hall of Memory, Birmingham's impressive war memorial. Created initially to pay tribute to those who gave their lives in the first world war, it has since served as a continuing memorial to local people lost in later conflicts. The Hall of Memory faces out onto an open space, towards the top of the photograph, flanked by Broad Street. This became known as Centenary Square in 1989, to celebrate the one hundredth anniversary of Birmingham's attainment of city status.

On the home front

Left: Lady Hillingdon, Deputy Chairman of the Women's Voluntary Service (WVS) appears to be examining the contents of this soyer boiler with delight. Although the words 'Drinking Water' are plain enough to see, it is probable that a few hundred morning 'cuppas' are boiling up in there. The occasion was the Civil Defence Combined Emergency Feeding Training Course and Exhibition at West Bromwich, on July 15th 1952. The smiling onlookers are other WVS stalwarts of No 9 region, from the left, Mrs Golding of Birmingham, Mrs Cozens of West Bromwich and Miss Gray, regional administrator. The last named in particular had a wealth of experience behind her, having joined WVS on its foundation in 1938 and, as the 'campaign' ribbons on her tunic show, having served in the Middle and Far East during World War II. The experience gained by Miss Gray and other WVS members in feeding bombed out families during the German 'blitz', or sustaining troops from mobile canteens in far-flung places, was invaluable to Civil Defence. The exercise in West Bromwich was designed to prepare for any emergency situation which would require the mass feeding of civilians, whether it arose from a natural disaster or a nuclear attack.

Above: The central feature in this picture is one of the famous improvised brick ovens, sometimes known as drum or dustbin ovens. WVS members were trained not only to use but also to build or assemble such items of field equipment as soyer boilers and dustbin ovens. Between 1939 and 1945 there had been plenty of material to practise with from the rubble of bombed houses! Wartime shortages had caused the appearance of the famous cartoon figure of Chad, peeping over a wall, with his perennial complaint of, 'Wot no ...?' In this case the WVS had chosen gas as the missing item, but the noticeboard exhorts people to make do with bricks and dustbins. 'Improvise' could well have been the one word motto of WVS. Lady Hillingdon watches with interest as the Mayoress of West Bromwich, Mrs Sower, places a joint of meat in the oven to roast. Amongst the onlookers are her husband the Mayor, Alderman H Sower, standing on the far left. Next to him is Mr J H Turner, Emergency Meals Officer. There is no doubt that this would not have been an empty exercise in that the WVS would have been facing the challenge of producing a full-scale meal, in the field, for several hundred people.

Below: This photograph may not relate to the Emergency Feeding Training Course at West Bromwich, in July 1952, but the transportable water carrier is part of the same theme - the rapid relay of essentials to any place where normal services have been disrupted. In this respect, too, Birmingham had 16 vans which could provide an Emergency Food Convoy - the Fast Food Squads. WVS uniform and insignia are much in evidence around the water carrier, especially the distinctive striped neckware, and the regional administrator for No 9 region, Miss Gray, stands at far left. Close to her, wearing a chain of office, is a very distinguished visitor, Lady Reading. With war imminent in 1938, it was she who was approached by the Home Secretary, Sir Samuel Hoare, with a view to recruiting women to help in Air Raid Precaution. Lady Reading founded WVS with a membership of five, which had mushroomed to 30,000 by the end of 1938. WVS would not become WRVS until 1966, when Queen Elizabeth II granted the addition of 'Royal'. It was less easy to recruit women to WVS in the 1950s as part of Civil Defence. Images of Hiroshima implanted a fatalistic belief that a nuclear war offered either death or a world that was not worth surviving in.

These ladies of the Women's Voluntary Service, No 9 region, are getting stuck in to the washing up with a will, and there would be plenty more to do that day. As participants in the Civil Defence exercise, 'Aspirin', on Sunday November 22nd 1953, not only did they have to provide tea and cake in the morning break, but they also had to provide a three course Sunday lunch for 400 guests! The exercise involved a Civil Defence Mobile Column coming to the rescue of local personnel under pressure from three 'incidents' at Grosvenor Street West, Lupin Street and Washwood Heath Road. With the 'Iron Curtain' dividing East and West Europe shortly after the end of World War II, and along with it the ever present fear of a nuclear war, Civil Defence was a priority for the government in the 1950s. Much experience had been gained in the war through Air Raid Precaution, and the associated activities of fire-fighting and ambulance work. The government was anxious to retain this pool of trained volunteers, and expand it if possible. Exercises such as 'Aspirin', one of several across the country at this time, helped to test the Civil Defence response in the face of a simulated nuclear bomb attack.

Although the WVS was an independent organisation, its members were well-equipped to don the armband of the Civil Defence Corps. Their recent experience of bringing emergency food supplies to victims of the German 'blitz' made them invaluable to Civil Defence. Not only this, in January 1953 gale force winds and exceptionally high tides had caused tremendous damage and some loss of life all along the East coast. As always, the WVS had responded magnificently. Viewed from this perspective, the WVS probably thought that feeding 400 people with a three course lunch, prepared in an emergency field kitchen, was nothing much to fuss about!

Nevertheless little problems did arise and the photograph shows WVS members, Mrs Rhodes and Mrs Hackett, discussing some of these with Emergency Meals Officer, Mr R S Pitts. The dome of the Hall of Memory, Birmingham's memorial to those lost in war, provides a suitably solemn backdrop to an exercise with such sombre undertones. Among those who enjoyed their Sunday lunch that day at the Cambridge Street Civic Restaurant were local dignitaries. Much praise was directed at the ingenuity of the WVS' cooking arrangements when the Deputy Lord and Lady Mayoress of Birmingham, Alderman and Mrs Bowen, inspected the equipment.

The prospect of a nuclear attack, and the destruction of essential public services in cities, was a terrifying one, but none the less a possibility. In that case, Civil Defence needed to be prepared. The Women's Voluntary Service (WVS) invariably played a part in these exercises on the emergency feeding side. The first picture [left] shows Mrs J H Bowden of No 9 region WVS keeping an eye on the apple tarts cooking in the ovens of the Bluff cooker, whilst Mr R A Bashford bastes the meat. He was Area Manager of Civic Restaurants and a Civil Defence Emergency Meals Instructor. Other WVS members Mrs Hackett to the left, and Mrs G Rhodes in the centre, take a keen interest in the proceedings. In the background the well-named Food Flying Squad stands ready. This consisted of four canteen vans, one water tanker and two stores vans. These vans, of a startling electric blue colour, were crewed by WVS volunteers. They were only one part of an Emergency Feeding Convoy of 16 vehicles for the Birmingham area, under the control of the Ministry of Food, which was said to be able to feed 8,000 people at a sitting.

Above (both pictures): It's all systems go on a dash to prepare a three course meal in a car park. The occasion was the Civil Defence exercise 'Aspirin', held on Sunday November 22nd 1953, and the cooking was being done on the Civic Centre Car Park, near Cambridge Street. This was one of the series of Civil Defence exercises being held around the country at this time, both to practise for a full-scale emergency situation, and to raise public awareness of Civil Defence. No sooner had World War II ended, in 1945, than Britain became involved in the Cold War with Russia.

The emergency feeding kitchen set up on the Civic Centre Car Park included three improvised brick cookers, sometimes known as dustbin or drum ovens. The picture above shows Mrs Rhodes and Mrs J Morgan about to place a large joint of meat inside one of these formidable cookers. These sturdy brick contraptions must have passed now into WVS folklore, along with the improvised brick hotplate stoves, as featured in the pictures. As one WVS member commented at the time, 'If you can cook on these, you can cook anywhere'. Nevertheless the hotplate stove is doing its duty by the brussel sprouts, and this time Mrs Bowden has the assistance of Mrs F Aston and Miss Beauvoisin.

Although Civil Defence armbands are prominent, the rest of the uniforms worn by the ladies are definitely WVS, particularly the headgear. There was very good reason for seeing WVS as an arm of Civil Defence because of the experience it had gained during World War II. The organisation was set up in 1938, when it was known that war was impending, with a view to involving women in Air Raid Precaution. WVS did sterling service in any number of ways - receiving evacuees, distributing clothing to bombed out families, knitting garments and providing mobile libraries for the armed services - but perhaps above all it had experience in providing nourishment

to people in difficult circumstances. It was not simply a matter of bringing food into air raid shelters either. After the disastrous Coventry air raids of 1940, plans were made for food convoys to go into badly blitzed areas and provide meals for people until services were working again. These Queen's Messenger Convoys, eighteen of them, were staffed by the WVS. Allied troops all over the world had good reason to give thanks for mobile WVS canteens which turned up, literally, anywhere.

Shopping spree

1950s High Street was a jostle of cars and pedestrians

Modern shopping centres may be comfortable and stylish, with a huge range of choice, but this photograph captures the flavour of city centre shopping as it used to be. High Street in July 1952 is one mad jostle of cars, delivery vans and pedestrians. A little dangerous - yes; but lively and friendly - definitely yes! There is no shortage of variety either. The shoppers can choose to buy shoes from Stylo, household goods from the long established Paul Taylor, or meat from that well-known name of Dewhurst. Even the pig looks happy at the prospect of everyone eating

'Hurrell's Dairyfeed Bacon'! The Board Inn is available for refreshment, but it has to be said that in the 1950s this would only have been of the liquid variety. Pubs had not yet entered the food industry, although you might have got a bag of Smith's Crisps (plain only) containing a little screw of salt in blue paper. If that does not bring back a few memories, then perhaps the sight of the gas lamp outside Paul Taylor's will. Wouldn't it be nice, just occasionally, to step outside the blandness of the shopping mall and back into the hustle and bustle of the old High Street?

Above: Day & Co was a local shoe retailer whose shop was a familiar sight on New Street for many years, and which ceased to do business only relatively recently. New Street has seen shops come and go over the course of a long history. In fact New Street is somewhat of a misnomer, for it is one of the Birmingham's oldest streets. The first certain reference to it is in a deed of 1397, and during the eighteenth century a swine market was held in New Street. The photograph of the charming young ladies gazing into the shop window was probably taken around 1950. The fashions on display seem to suggest this, especially the 'peep-toe' shoes belonging to one of the girls. Added to this, there are several copies of that memorable old magazine, 'Picture Post', in the window priced at 4d (1 1/2 p.) Clearly Day & Co were doing a promotion on 'Joyce' shoes. The brand name is visible on the bottom shelf, and across one copy of 'Picture Post' it mentions a 'Joyce' advertisement within. The rapt attention of the girls, however, seems to be fixed on the rather simplistic design of a church, but no doubt this was all tied in with the promotion.

Right: A sight to strike fear into the heart of the stoutest man. Such was the scene outside the C&A department store on Corporation Street, in January 1953, as women queued up for the New Year sales. One man has paused to take a glance, but the rest are wisely hurrying on, for who would have dared to get in the way of any of these women hell-bent on securing a bargain? The men in the middle of the throng were probably trapped! People are much more blasé about big store sales now, for they tend to go on the year round, but in the 1950s the New Year sales were a special event. Overnight queuing for the really 'hot' bargains was not unusual, and when the doors were thrown open at 9am, it was not a place for the faint-hearted. The press would delight in reporting stories of women rampaging through stores like the avenging hordes of Attila the Hun. No doubt it was much exaggerated, and the women on this photograph appear to be a friendly and civilised bunch. It is interesting to note how important headgear is for locating particular era. The hats on view, especially the number of headscarves, make this definitely a 50s setting.

Some market names stand the test of time and two such are pictured here in this shot of the 1950s. At the junction of Corporation Street and Bull Street we find Lewis's and Dolcis, familiar names for 'Brummy' shoppers for years to come, although Lewis's closed in 1991. It is certainly a busy time of day as shoppers flood across the streets.

At this date the austerity of the war years was a very recent memory, but shopping was not yet the leisure activity that it would increasingly become from the 1960s. Some aspects of rationing still remained until 1954. Therefore the range of goods was limited as compared to later years, as was the money available to spend. It was not quite 'shop

'til you drop' in the 50s. The line of cars on the right, seemingly waiting on the starting grid and raring to go, gives a hint of a problem that would only worsen in the years to come - that of inner city traffic congestion. The existence of a one-way system was a recognition that city centre traffic had to be subject to some controls, but this was only a precursor to much harsher measures later.

A glance at the 1950s

MELODY MAKERS
Few teenage girls could resist the blatant sex-appeal of 'Elvis the Pelvis', though their parents were scandalised at the moody Presley's provocatively gyrating hips. The singer took America and Britain by storm with such hits as 'Jailhouse Rock', 'All Shook Up' and 'Blue Suede Shoes'. The rhythms of Bill Haley and his Comets, Buddy Holly, Chuck Berry, and Roy Orbison (who had a phenomenal three-octave voice) turned the 1950s into the Rock 'n' Roll years.

INVENTION AND TECHNOLOGY
Until the late 1950s you did not carry radios around with you. Radios were listened to at home, plugged into a mains socket in every average sitting room. Japan was in the forefront of electronic developments even then, and in 1957 the Japanese company Sony introduced the world's very first all-transistor radio - an item of new technology that was small enough to fit into your pocket. The major consumer product caught on fast - particularly with teenage listeners.

SCIENCE AND DISCOVERY
DNA (deoxyribonucleic acid) was first defined as long ago as 1953, and the effects have been far-reaching. The key discovery was developed over the following years and today DNA fingerprinting has become an accepted part of life. Genetic diseases such as haemophilia and cystic fibrosis have been identified. Criminals are continually detected and brought to justice. Biological drugs have been developed. More controversially, drought and disease-resistant plants have been engineered - and Dolly the sheep has been produced.

At work

Above: The Bull Ring development is in its initial stages here, back in the early 1960s. Looking across to St Martin's Church, and a widened Digbeth High Street, the whole scene is in that depressing stage of any development where it resembles a bomb site. Nothing much is left of the old; nothing recognisable has yet emerged of the new. The only real advantage seems to be the appearance of lots of free, if temporary, parking space. It might well have been the second world war that brought about the end of the old Bull Ring, not so much because German bombing on the night of August 25th/26th 1940 reduced the Market Hall to an empty shell, but because the war changed so many social habits and attitudes. The new Bull Ring was simply one aspect of the 'brave new world' that post-war planners in all spheres tried to create. As early as 1940 Henry Manzoni had drawn up proposals for an inner ring road, and a redeveloped Bull Ring was part of them. It took 20 years for the scheme to get off the drawing board, and the old Bull Ring vanished for ever. The Market Hall was just one of the landmarks to perish, being replaced by the Manzoni Gardens.

Above right: 'War is the midwife of revolution', proclaimed Lenin, in 1917. If this picture of the Civic Restaurant on Cambridge Street, around the end of World War II, doesn't look to have a particularly revolutionary flavour, well in a sense it did. This was a British Restaurant, sponsored by the government, and was a symbol of a social revolution brought about by the war. Life in cities was so disrupted by bombing, evacuation and war-work that the normal pattern of eating at home was destroyed for many. From 1941 the Ministry of Food took on emergency powers for serving food in air raid shelters. Along with this came a concern for nutrition, and experts were called in to advise about such matters as a balanced diet. After all, the war could best be won on the Home Front by a healthy nation. By July 1943 over 2000 British Restaurants were in existence, serving a meat dish, a sweet and a cup of tea or coffee, for around 1s 2d (6p). British Restaurants gradually disappeared after the war, but their nutritional values were carried on by works canteens and school dinner services, along with the idea that the eating habits of the nation should be of some concern to the government.

Flights of Birmingham, 80 years of coaching

To be trained by Daimler was a passport to employment in any motor business. Frank Flight with true 'Brummie' independence decided to be his own boss and, in 1913, set up a taxi service and garage next to his house at 83 Victoria Road, Aston. Business was going well when the Serbs triggered off The Great War. Frank Flight, a 'Terrier' Sergeant, was posted from his unit's Summer Camp on Salisbury Plain to defend 'Little Belgium'. He sensibly sold two of his taxis as there was a shortage of civilian male drivers.

In 1916 he received his 'Blighty One', a wound worthy of repatriation to a military hospital in Colchester. During his convalescence he planned to buy an army ambulance at the end of the war and convert it to dual purpose use. When fit he was posted to the Daimler works to build the revolutionary fighting vehicles, code named 'Tanks' to confuse enemy spies! He spent the rest of the war fighting in France as one of the new breed of mechanised soldiers.

On his return home he married Emily Louise (Amy) Adams who became not only the valuable helpmate so vital to every family business but the mother of Marjorie and Frank Kenneth. Frank Senior bought his war surplus ambulance which he converted, as planned, into a dual purpose carrier. During the week he undertook parcels deliveries and furniture removals while at weekends he changed the van body for a coach body in which to carry trippers. As the business expanded he bought more taxis, dropped the van carrying element and increased the coaching business, in 1922, by buying two Daimler coaches.

His brother Norman spent a brief period with him after which Frank bought 114 Victoria Road, a few houses along from his home, which had space for a larger garage. In the 1920s he competed with the Corporation bus services by running Flight's buses from the city centre to Witton, Perry Barr and Kingstanding. During the Great Strike of 1926 he had to run the gauntlet of striking bus crews by driving full pelt through a picket line. The police protected his garage, now equipped with five coaches, from attack. From 1928 private enterprise buses were banned in Birmingham so the Flights concentrated on taxis, private hire and coach trips with all the office work being done by Amy Flight.

In 1939 the well established firm was enjoying deserved success with a fleet of five coaches and ten taxis/private hire cars. Came the war and a number of coaches were stripped out to facilitate the rapid issue of gas masks to civilians who entered at one end and left at the other after a brief lesson in handling and use. All the coaches were then commandeered for military use and the

Top right: *The Victoria Road premises pictured in the early 1930s.*
Left: *Two taxis in the mid 1920s.*

Above: *An Austin Landaulette available to hire for weddings and outings pictured in the mid 1920s.*
Left: *A young Ken Flight outside the premises in the mid 1930s.*

taxis converted, half for use as ambulances and half for towing fire fighting equipment. Any drivers not 'called up' into the Forces were trained as Auxiliary Fire Fighters while Amy became a Fire Service administrator.

Due to the proximity of armaments factories such as BSA and Castle Bromwich, home of the legendary Spitfire, Aston received unwelcome visits from enemy bombers. In 1940 the family were saved by one of the corrugated iron Anderson Shelters during an air raid which damaged both home and garage. Frank commanded a group of 'Specials', unpaid part-time police, throughout the war. He frequently picked up the smaller incendiary bombs which he carried in his car boot to a bomb disposal unit! The family left war torn Aston for a house in Four Oaks as wartime restrictions hindered the repair of the garage and the absence of his commandeered coaches prevented any other vehicular work.

By 1943 two of the commandeered coaches were returned which, with a third, were employed to ferry the Spitfire builders between safe lodgings in Tamworth and the Castle Bromwich factory. Other Birmingham coach owners, whose businesses had not been commandeered, expanded greatly with such war work while the Flights had only three of their coaches returned by a grateful government. Somehow another coach was obtained on the suspension of hostilities and despite continued petrol rationing Flight's business began to grow once more.

The first new coach for almost ten years was purchased in 1947, followed by two in 1949. On his demobilisation from the RAF Ken took over from his father and obtained a licence to operate Express Coach services, excursions and coach tours. An excited public queued for coach outings to anywhere out of town, Mystery Tours were then very popular. Ken wed Gwendoline Horton who left Four Oaks to work in the company office and to set up home in a flat over the garage. They moved to Streetly between the births of their children Sheila Ann and Frank Geoffrey. Their five coaches were AEC Burlinghams then the best available, as part of Ken's drive to reach the top.

He persuaded Aston Villa FC, for twenty years a client of Flight's taxis, to travel by coach in the future. Maybe this luxurious travel helped the Villa win the FA Cup in 1957? Since that happy occasion Flights have ferried the Villa and, more recently, West Bromwich Albion and other football clubs to all their away matches. Flights bought four first class coach companies in the 1960s, one of which was famed for inclusive tour programmes. Rapid expansion during the 1960s led to coach holidays and express services along the new M1 in the ultimate of comfort and safety.

Above: *All aboard a 1928 Daimler for a day out in the early 1930s.* *Below:* *Another Daimler ready to depart in 1932.*

In the 1960s new, longer models of the luxurious AEC coaches were added to the fleet which was taking travellers abroad for all-inclusive coach holidays. Flights noticed that the type of business which had been so successful up until the early 1970s was beginning to decline. A car owning public was looking for holiday independence and a flexibility not available on coach tours. Flights met this change with their customary adaptability based on the realisation that mass air travel was the mode for the future. In 1975 an application was made to the Department of Transport and the British Airports Authority for a licence to operate daily coaches in and out of London Heathrow Airport. This move was fiercely fought against by other coach firms in Birmingham until after some 18 months Flights won their case and commenced operating the new FlightLink service.

It took time for travellers to appreciate the excellent and, above all, totally reliable door to door service. Eventually FlightLink got airborne as it earned a solid reputation with travel agents and grew to running 24 return services every day carrying nearly half a million travellers per year. The 'Next Stop' was the South of France and Spain where Flight's Supersun Holidays operated holidays in tents, mobile homes and apartments in the 1970s and 80s. Travel was by state of the art double decker coaches, with superb catering facilities superior to any others.

This lucrative trade was affected by de-regulation in the mid 1980s intended to open coaching to all comers. As a result many underfunded small operators using rather older coaches, hired for each journey, undercut prices below a sensible margin. Flights decided to reduce their commitment to this end of the market and concentrate on more lucrative touring work and eventually the mobile homes and apartments were sold. During this period Sheila Flight, on leaving school, joined the family travel agency and reservations department. She worked her way through the company until she took over the Conference Company which has been her highly successful career ever since.

In 1979 she wed Paul Wheeler by whom she has two sons Stephen and Jamie. Her brother, Frank Geoffrey, trained as an accountant before entering the family firm of which he is now the Group Managing Director. He married Noreen Friel in 1992 and they have a son Frank George and a daughter Scarlett May. Geoffrey was born with his share of the family drive, efficiency and enthusiasm which has seen Flights adapt successfully to the mixed fortunes of life in the 20th Century. The opening of the NEC on the Coventry Road east

Left: Three Burlingham Seagulls off to Wembley to return with the 1957 FA Cup and the Aston Villa team. Below: The Berners Street premises in 1961.

of Birmingham led to Flights entering the specialist field of corporate ground handling operations with the high profile national and international events being staged there. Today Flight's Coach Travel provide all the on-site transport on behalf of the NEC with a fleet of dedicated low-floor buses.

Growth was such that the premises occupied since the 1960s were no longer adequate. It was difficult to find a site large enough to accommodate the coaches in a location where planning permits for twenty-four hour operations would be granted. Bristol Street Motors saved the day by selling their Beacon House, Long Acre service depot of four and a half acres in Aston which Flights bought in 1994. From this new base the company operates all its existing ventures plus a new division, Flight's Motor Services Ltd., to utilise the excellent maintenance facilities.

In 1996 the highly successful FlightLink business was sold to National Express who then contracted Flights to continue operating much of the expanded airport service! Fifty five coaches and the business of Excelsior Holidays, one of Britain's premier touring firms, were bought in 1997 together with a clutch of travel agencies in Excelsior's home territory of the south of England.

Flight's Excelsior Holidays offers an unchallengeable selection of coach holidays all over the UK and Europe.

The Flight's fleet of coaches is light years away from the converted military ambulance run by the first Frank Flight. The 32 seat VIP Sovereign coach provides mobile corporate hospitality facilities second to none. Business guests can be fed and watered in style complete with silver service on the move or in an attractive location. Customers can utilise the on board fax, satellite, PC links and Data telephone services comparable to anything operated by ocean liners or 'trains de luxe'. Their luxurious Advantage Chauffeur Services provide impressive transport for all aspects of travel from personal airport links, via sight-seeing and corporate entertainment, to a day at Royal Ascot by luxury car.

By dint of hard work and professionalism by all 350 members of the Flight's team from administrators to coach captains and drivers, from maintenance staff to travel agents, the company has become the third largest coach operator in the UK. For comfort, safety and pleasurable travel take flight with Flights overland.

Top: *A 1972 Plaxton AEC outside Aston Hall.*
Above: *Just three of the fleet at the company headquarters in 1998.*

The company whose products fit 'The Bill'

In 1780 a certain Mr Hiat entered his name indelibly into manufacturing history when he opened a factory at No. 26 Masshouse Lane, Birmingham. Little is now known for certain about Mr Hiat beyond his name and the fact that he made 'prisoners' handcuffs, felons' leg irons, gang chains and nigger collars'; however, we can also surmise that he was a remarkably far-sighted businessman, as the specialist business he founded has survived virtually unchanged in both name and nature for more than two centuries.

Public taste has brought about some refinements; for instance, nigger collars and gang chains have not figured on the company's catalogues for many a year, though in the days of deportation, the Slave Trade and the French Revolution these would have been in great demand. A man who, for whatever reason, was unfortunate enough to end up in chains in those days could expect little sympathy. It was the practice for prisoners' collars and shackles to be fastened not with expensive locks which could be picked, but with rivets; written records from the mid-19th century describe a Midlands convict, Bilston collier 'Black' Jack Hollis, bending over an anvil while the prison blacksmith rivetted a collar round Black Jack's neck with a hammer.

Various restraints were required by the Admiralty, the War Office and the Foreign Office during the 19th century, and there was a steady export trade to the USA; New York's police force became a regular client. Some items, too, would have been bought by travelling merchants and traders who would then have sold them throughout the colonies and the other parts of the world which they visited. During the 1950s a director of Hiatt was rather surprised when, during a trip to Italy, he went on a guided tour of an ancient castle and happened to notice the inscription 'Hiat' on a pair of leg-irons in the dungeon; the cause of his surprise was not the fact that Hiat had made the leg-irons, but the guide's claim they were over 500 years old!

Hiat, or Hiatt as the name was later spelt, occupied the original factory at Masshouse Lane for more than 150 years, employing skilled metalworkers to manufacture components in wrought cast iron, for assembly by hand by skilled handcuff fitters whose art lay in selecting, by eye, parts that would fit together with a minimum of filing, so as to maintain a speedy output. The first Trade Directory record of Hiat's dates back to 1832. It is doubtful whether the Hiat family had any connection with the firm at that time, but the name was known all over the world. In this country, the first British police force, established in London following an Act of Parliament passed in 1829 and nicknamed 'The Peelers', obtained its first handcuffs from Hiatt's; indeed 'The Old Bill', as London's Metropolitan Police is sometimes politely known today, still uses the same supplier.

Below: *An advertisement from the late 19th century.*

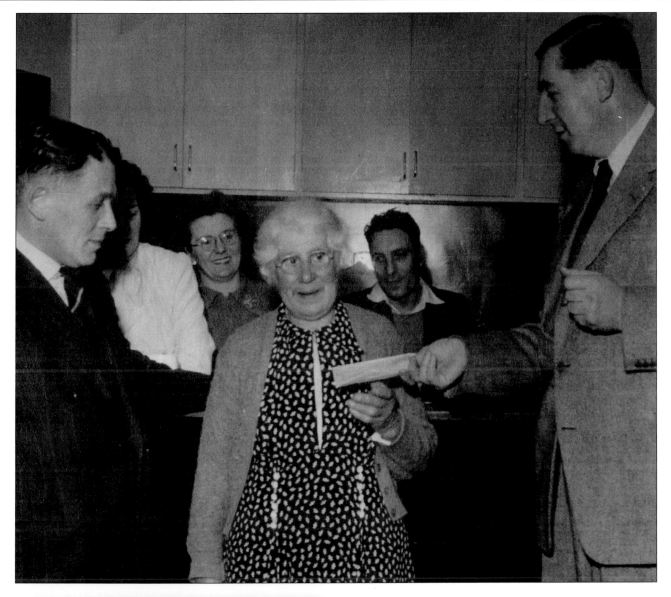

crowd into towns and cities which had no proper housing for them. One 19th century addition to the Hiatt's range was the barrel-lock handcuffs which are still produced today.

The first suggestion of a variation in product range comes during the second half of the 19th century; the manufacture of restraints for humans continued, but restraints for animals were added as a sideline - principally 'bull-leading devices' and nose rings for bulls and pigs. The coming of the first world war put the focus firmly back onto devices for humans, however. During the war the handcuff makers worked from seven in the morning to nine at night to keep up with demand, while civil unrest in the years between the wars continued to keep them busy, with a brisk trade during the Colliers' Strike of 1921 and policemen queuing all the way down Masshouse Lane in the General Strike of 1926 to collect handcuffs, whistles and truncheons.

Handcuffs have remained an essential tool in the maintenance of law and order since deteriorating social conditions set the urban trend for rising crime during the industrial revolution, when the workforce had to

Top: *Louisa Goodman on her retirement in 1953, presented by the then MD, Harry La Trobe.*
Above left: *Thomas Froggatt, who worked for the company for over 70 years and made handcuffs for Houdini.*

One of Hiatt's few competitors was Thos Froggatt & Co. Thomas Froggatt had reputedly begun making handcuffs when he was ten years old; he was a long-time personal friend of Houdini and had made many of the sets of handcuffs from which the escapologist escaped - and one set of leg-irons from which he could not escape, simply because they were so restrictive that once they were attached he could not reach the lock. In 1937 Thos Froggatt was taken over by Hiatt; Mr Froggatt was by this time 73 years old, so may have been contemplating retirement, but in fact he was to make handcuffs for the company for another eleven years, commuting daily from his home in the Cotswolds to the centre of Birmingham.

The prospect of another war brought Hiatt's activities to national prominence again, and the firm stepped up production of whistles, and of the rattles and handbells which were to signal the possible presence of poison gas, the former giving the warning and the latter the 'all clear'. However, Masshouse Lane, right in the centre of Birmingham, was not a comfortable place to be once bombing started; the frequent prolonged night raids and shorter attacks during the day made it inevitable that, sooner or later, the factory would be hit, and on the night of April 9th 1941 it was. A shower of incendiary bombs destroyed virtually the whole of the area, although a gallant young fire-watcher armed with a Fire Brigade pump and hosepipe managed to stop the fire consuming Hiatt's machine shop where the most valuable tools were kept. The following day the homeless company was able to come to an arrangement with Fan Disc Limited in Northwood Street, whereby it could move into part of Fan Disc's premises; and a

month later Hiatt was in full production again. Hiatt remained at 109 Northwood Street for the duration of the war; then in 1947 the firm was able to acquire one and a half acres of freehold land at Baltimore Road, in the suburb of Great Barr. A new factory was built, to a design by the well-known Birmingham architect Leonard J Multon, which the company still occupies at the the time of writing. This purpose-built workshop, with its long, low, streamlined frontage, is in itself of architectural interest as an admirable example of post-war industrial aesthetics, though a complete contrast to the fascinating mid-18th century factory in Masshouse Lane which had been Hiatt's home for more than a century and a half.

It was when the firm moved out to Great Barr that Mr Froggatt, aged 84, decided that the extra travelling distance was just a little too much, and he decided to retire. Another long-serving employee some ten years his junior was Louisa Goodman, who had started work at Hiatt's in 1886 at the age of 11; she stayed with the firm when it moved, and when she retired in 1953 at the age of 78 a special ceremony was held to mark the occasion.

Hiatt set up another sideline in its new factory, which represented the firm's biggest diversification ever. It invested in two injection moulding machines and two special moulds, and became the first manufacturer in England to make a plastic cable clip. Once again the company had succeeded in identifying a niche in the market and making the perfect product to fit it; with the

Above: *Hiatt's inspection and warehouse c1950.*

growth in the electrical and television industry, there was a continual demand for these clips. Output began at 20,000 cable clips per week, and by 1978 30 injection moulding machines using 40 special moulds housed in a separate 12,000 square foot factory were producing 4,000,000 cable clips a week. In that year the Plastic Division was sold as a separate entity, and Hiatt returned to its traditional focus of restraints and related items.

Close liaison with police forces and other organisations over the years has enabled the company to adapt its product range to meet requirements. A glance through past catalogues and records shows the extreme ingenuity of some of Hiatt's designs, and also gives a modern reader some intriguing insights into the little everyday problems and customs of times gone by. For instance, it appears that the original Metropolitan Police Lantern occasionally spilled oil onto an officer's clothing when held down, and to eliminate this problem an Improved Metropolitan design was introduced,

incorporating a new patent oil vessel which stopped any oil escaping. The Improved version was slightly more expensive, at 78/- a dozen (£3.90 in today's currency) as opposed to 70/4 a dozen (£3.51) for the original model. There even seems to have been an element of the status symbol about a policeman's handcuffs; ordinary Police Spring Grips were 8/- a pair, but promotion to Superintendent presumably entitled the officer to Superintendent's Light Steel Grips at 12/- a pair. As recently as 1972 Hiatt's range of uniform accessories and badges included Licensed Hawkers' Badges issued by Manchester Corporation, as well as belts, armlets, whistles, helmet plates, chrome plated numerals, chrome plated badges for caps, collars and button holes, and buttons, either horn or chrome plated, with button brushes and button sticks to keep them shiny.

Other early products which illustrate the company's versatility include steel toys, dog collars and chains,

Below: The company's assembly shop c1950.

hammers and lunatic locks; and a newspaper article from 1948 refers to the firm having in the past manufactured scold bridles, which apparently consisted of a rough bit which went into the mouth to keep the tongue still, while bridle locked at the back of the head.

In July 1984 the company was acquired by Geoffrey Cross, the present Managing Director, when it was in need of revitalisation. Since then, the company has regained its position as the World's leading quality handcuff manufacturer with the largest range, and enjoys some 90 per cent of the home market where principal customers include police forces, prisons, Customs & Excise, MoD security organisations and airlines. Quality has always been Hiatt's priority; competitors may offer inferior products at a lower price, but law enforcement professionals regard Hiatt's handcuffs as the best in the world, and Hiatt's superior product design and engineering excellence have won them the custom of NATO, the United Nations Security Forces and many other customers throughout the world. Having been involved in the export trade from its very

early days, the firm now supplies virtually every police force in the world, as well as the various security organisations who are responsible for protecting Royal families and world leaders in North and South America, Europe, Scandinavia, Australasian and the Middle East, Asia and various African countries. The company's constant search for new markets continues, and took the current Chairman to Armenia on a memorable trip during which he was shot at by local gangsters, and was treated by his hosts to a local delicacy consisting of a very private portion of a bull's anatomy, served with a knob of butter. It is not recorded which of these two experiences he enjoyed the least.

The unique specialist knowledge of the industry which Hiatts has built up over the centuries is reflected in its current range of handcuffs, which is more comprehensive than that of any other manufacturer. The

Above: *An advertisement from the early 1970s.*
Below: *An exhibition in the 1950s of the company's earliest works.*

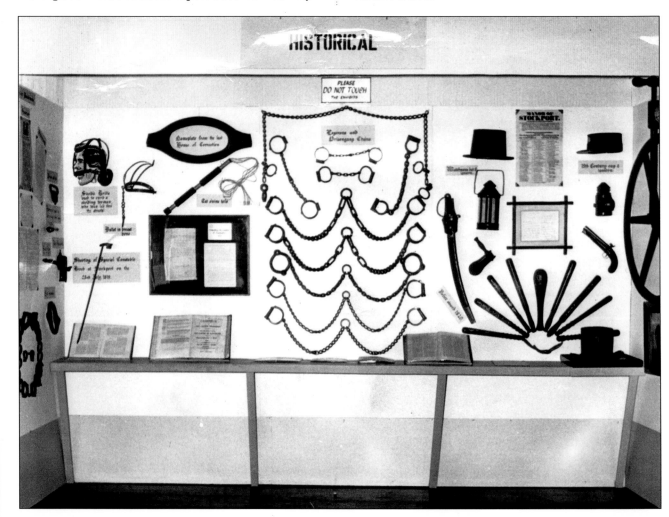

*Top: The premises in the 1950s. **Left:** Today's products. **Below:** Mr Geoffrey Cross, the current Managing Director demonstrating the 'ultimate handcuff'.*

locking handcuff for which there is considerable world demand will be launched in June 1999.

While today's offenders might wish that Hiatt had been a little less adept at designing strong, secure and swiftly-applied handcuffs, they can at least console themselves by considering how much more comfortable they are than their 19th century counterparts. Not only are modern handcuffs attractively finished in a choice of satin or black, with the edges machined smoothly so as to avoid scratching the miscreant's skin, but they also have up to 22 locking positions to accommodate large and small wrists equally snugly. So, although today's offender has no more chance of escaping from his handcuffs than Black Jack Hollis had from his neck collar, at least he is spared the agony of wondering whether his head will be smashed in by the blacksmith's hammer as he closes that rivet . . . and, for once, he may

obvious qualities to look for in a pair of handcuffs are those which make it strong and pick-proof, and Hiatts' products certainly meet these criteria. The official quality standards in this case are those laid down by the United States National Institute of Justice, which have also been adopted by the United Kingdom Home Office, and these standards are met or exceeded by all Hiatts' steel-based models, which are today manufactured principally in carbon steel, but also in aluminium and mazak castings. However, another very important consideration is the speed with which the handcuffs can be affixed, and this has become imperative in recent years when the number of violent situations which the police are called upon to deal with has risen dramatically. Swift restraint of criminals is the best way of preventing them from inflicting injury, and to this end Hiatt's modern range of rigid 'snap-on' handcuffs all incorporate the firm's unique backloading feature for speed cuffing; the company has also produced a training video showing basic speedcuffing techniques. The latest addition to the range is Hiatt's 'Ultimate' handcuff, the world's only folding rigid handcuff which is very compact to carry, and a new high-security individual

well echo the law enforcer's praise of a unique company which has pioneered the development of their particular product for more than 200 years and which is today as forward-looking and innovative as ever and planning a move to state-of-art-premises which are currently under construction.

Leading the way in fashion and style

Remember the advertising jingle that brought Lee Longland so successfully to mind? The elegant, tempting and inspiring shop that appeals to home makers of all ages and purses. Anyone privileged to study the catalogues produced in each decade looks back through a history of taste and quality. In some generations the changes are few, in others they are astonishing. What does come through is the ability of a long established Birmingham furnishing store to reflect the styles, wealth and personal needs of each era. We all have memories of visiting Lee Longland in Broad Street on the edge of fashionable Edgbaston but what came before?

Lee Longlands came into being as the fulfilment of a dream shared by two men working for someone else. In the palmy days of the 'Edwardian Summer' Robert Lee and George Longland were both employed by the well established firm of Chamberlain, King and Jones. They discovered a shared ambition and ideas and, bravely choosing to compete against Chamberlains of Birmingham, went into partnership and started their own business.

Their first shop in 1902 was in Broad Street on a site now occupied by the Lloyds TSB building. Like the famous Liberty shop in London the Lee Longlands store had a black and white timber facade, to many customers an indication of longevity and worth. The wagon arch led to the stabling at the rear of the store which provided the horse power for deliveries. Maintaining such facilities was the normal choice for all the better shops as well groomed horse flesh, sparkling harness and smartly painted wagons were an excellent advertising medium in an age when people appreciated 'a smart turnout'.

The stock in trade of those gracious days reflected the wealth of the city at the heart of the country whose empire spanned the world. Lee Longlands advertised as 'Artistic House Furnishers' to a clientele influenced not only by the Pre-Raphaelites and the Birmingham Arts

Top left: *Robert Lee, co-founder of the company.*
Left: *George Longland, co-founder of the company.*
Below: *The cabinet workroom of the original shop in the early 1900s.*

Movement but increasingly attracted by the cleaner lines expounded by Charles Rennie Mackintosh and others of that ilk. The discerning shopper could furnish their home from top to bottom, although furnishing the 'Below Stairs' domain was neglected by some, but by no means all, employers of domestic staff. The store, which also held stocks of antique furniture to cater for the English love of old pieces, supplied the very latest in modern design, some made in the firm's workshops, for every room in the house. Textiles, then as now, included ranges of carpets, curtains and soft furnishings of all kinds. In addition Lee Longlands provided re-make services for bedding

Top: *The original premises which opened in 1902.* **Left:** *A fine display of dining furniture in the original shop.*

Hurley Robinson, whose plans for an extra fifth floor were scotched by World War Two. The present four storey store, built of brick clad with handsome Portland stone, was proudly opened to the public on 9th September 1931. It was advertised as a modern building, well lit and centrally heated but staffed in the Lee Longland tradition by staff who knew current vogues, their stock, and, who could listen to and guide their clients. Today the code of practice remains the same, to provide customers,

and re-upholstery. The firm also undertook decorating, both interior and exterior, by highly skilled craftsmen and removals, too, for those changing house. By 1912, the ten year old business had invested in a motor delivery van, a splendid Darracq with solid rubber tyres, with which to impress 'Brummies' with the visible message that Lee Longlands were as bang up to date as the latest 'Musical show' or 'Dixieland Ragtime Melody'.

Another innovation introduced by the partners was 'Payment out of Income', a hire purchase scheme to help younger customers. The store was also the first in Birmingham to illuminate shop windows, by the electric light, after closing time. The first world war finished for ever the world for which the store then catered. The second generation, Robert Lee and Herbert Lee together with Gilbert Longland served in the Army, as did many of the family's employees including the skilled cabinet makers. They returned to help guide the business through the inter-war years when their catalogues show styles very similar to the Scandinavian styles fashionable in the 1950s! In 1931 the founders purchased a larger site further up Broad Street, at its junction with Granville Street. They commissioned an architect and within six months the building was completed according to the plans of Birmingham architect A.

Top left: The bedroom furnishing department prior to 1914. Right: The new shop at 224 Broad Street which opened in 1931.

whether their family are 'old clients' or not, with the best of advice in making them feel at home both in the shop and in the customer's own home, tastefully furnished by Lee Longlands. In the 1930s the clean simple lines of Art Deco furniture were displayed in mock up 'Flats' in the store, an indication of the increasing number of people moving into flats. Those unable to cope without living-in domestic staff found the concept of service flats, which then provided cleaning services and meals either in the restaurant or delivered to your flat, the ultimate in Modern Living.

For the second time in a generation war in 1939 interrupted the lives of everyone in the country as craftsmen and sales staff were called up into the forces or essential war work. Strictly rationed supplies of materials were matched by a decline in demand for top quality

Today as always, Lee Longland set out to help their customers by supplying goods on deferred terms. These enable home owners to budget out of income for furniture which they can enjoy the use of as soon as the deposit has been paid. Midlanders can choose to shop either in the original Birmingham store, which is now a listed building, or visit the new Lee Longlands store in the refurbished Regency Arcade in Royal Leamington Spa. The latter has been restored to its earlier glory with a glass lift to complement the classical exterior and elegant iron balustrades of the era. For shoppers in the Cotswolds, the handsome former spa town of Cheltenham also has a Lee Longlands shop. This is located a short distance from the town centre on the Bath Road beyond the Gentlemen's College. Local people have long regarded the Bath Road as a convenient shopping street in town with easy parking and sensible prices.

In the early 1900s the 'Carriage Trade' customers expected shop managers to bring goods out to their homes for inspection! In the late 1990s the much more democratic carriage trade prefer to park their cars within a few minutes walk of the shops they patronise. Each of the Lee Longlands stores offers customers the facility of nearby car parking to add to their other services. The third and fourth generation of both families are still actively involved today with the Midland's premier furnishing department stores. For customers with the ultimate in taste Lee Longlands is the place to satisfy it with sound quality at a fair price.

Top left: The 'Winchcombe' dining-set, an example of the minimalist furnishing styles from the 1930s. *Above left:* Selling furniture in the 1970s. **Below:** Some of today's furniture on display in the 'Grange' studio, just one of many collections of furniture that cater for all kinds of tastes.

furniture. The excellent Utility furniture was allowed only to those recently married or replacing a bombed out home. The store itself was requisitioned by the Ministry of Food to cache supplies of dried fish, dried milk and the unforgettable dried eggs. Lee Longlands, somehow, kept going in a small part of it selling acres of 'Black Out' material and other utilitarian goods allowed by the Ministry of Supply.

Once rationing ended there was an explosive desire to boot out old ideas and refurbish homes and lifestyles as quickly and as colourfully as could be afforded. The 1951 'Festival of Britain', or Contemporary, look was 'in' with its simplicity of design and clean basic colour schemes imported from Scandinavia. Polished woods, woven fabrics and hand made pottery were all regarded as new, just as they had been when introduced in the 1890s by William Morris. Today modern 'teens crave for the styles adopted by their parents in their youth. Any store with the capacity to buy rejected styles could make a mint selling them to the next generation of fashion leaders!

No job too small, no distance too far

Divorce, death and removal are said to be the most trying of times for families. By the time the divorce court looms it is often too late to do anything other than accept the situation. There's not much we can do about dying, either. When you've got to go, you've got to go. But moving house is another question all together. It may be another case of when you've got to go once more, but this time you have some control. Having found your new home and the solicitor to sort out the legal work for you, all that remains is to book a reliable company to move your belongings. It is no good trying to do it yourself. There are too many 'Right said Freds' who rick backs, scratch antiques and strain marriages trying to do it themselves. Why use professionals to do the selling, buying and legal stuff and then trust an amateur with your most valued possessions? This is where a company such as White's Removals and Transport Ltd comes into its own. This is no Johnny come lately form of company. In 1998, it celebrated its centenary. A century of experience to be drawn upon is not to be sneezed at. How many thousands of armchairs have been moved, how many millions of books have been carried and how many cups of tea drunk in that time? It hardly bears thinking about. Yet, it is that very experience that inspires confidence. With it comes the gratitude of the satisfied customer who will act as the best advert any company can get - personal recommendation. There must have been

plenty of those since 1898, as the company has gone from strength to strength since those late Victorian days.

The founder, JF White, had worked in the removal trade before trying his luck on his own, so he was no novice when it came to dealing with the public and moving their house contents from one home to another. But it is a big step to go it alone and there were times when he wondered whether or not he had done the right thing. However, with the perseverance of the Victorian, he was determined to succeed. If he could have visualised the business as it is today, he was a far sighted man. Working in and around the Birmingham area, Mr White was a familiar sight leaving the yard of 35 Cromwell Street, Nechells to start his day moving some excited family on its way to a new challenge and adventure. The transport was, of course, provided in those times by one horse-drawn dray. Removals might have meant more than one journey for both man and beast. Hail, rain or shine would find Mr White above a pair of sturdy Shires, his feet on the duckboard calling to his charges and clicking their reins. How would he have regarded the air conditioned cabins and smooth ride of the vehicles of to-day? Would he have thought of them as a luxury or turned up his nose at the soft living of the modern removal man? All we can say is that the employees of this age would not trade places for a gold clock.

Although a removal business, White's has never had to move itself very far. It has continued to operate from Nechells throughout its entire existence. The premises have changed, but the

Above: *The original horse drawn vehicle.*
Left: *The original steam driven removal lorry. The driver would have to get up at 4 o'clock to get the steam up ready for the off at 8 o'clock.*

Left: White's moving the City of Birmingham Symphony Orchestra. Below: The original premises on Oliver Street.

from the days of the dray. These days huge vans sweep along the motorways across the length and breadth of the country. It is not just this country that sees them, either. White's is now a truly international operation. If you stuck a pin into the globe it is almost certain that White's Removals and Transport have arranged to convey some house contents, office furniture or other goods to that destination. The firm is particularly well known in South Africa, India and Australia.

locality has not. Consequently, a steady client base has been established and families have come back to White's, 'the removal people' time and again to use the service they have come to rely on. After Cromwell Street, it was on Oliver Street that the business continued to prosper. The current base of operations is to be found at 257 Great Lister Street. It is here that you can appreciate the size of the venture. When the company came to these premises in the 1950s it occupied 8,000 sq ft. Now there are no fewer than 31,000 sq ft of space. Every inch is needed and is fully utilised. It is certainly a far cry

As well as the usual house moves, business is heavy in the removal and storage of archives and files. Solicitors often use the company's services for this purpose. Sitting in a small legal office somewhere in the city centre, a solicitor's clerk will be looking at a pile of ancient documents that are no use to man nor beast. Collecting dust, they are using space that could be freed for a better use. What is the answer?

Send for White's. Accountants anguishing over a load of bankrupt stock will wonder what to do with it whilst the creditors' meetings are continuing and the premises sealed. What is the answer? Send for White's. Even the ordinary householder wanting to store his possessions as he moves out of one house and waits for the next one to be ready knows the answer. Send for White's. Storage is provided in containerised units. Clients are happy in the knowledge that everything is under lock and key in the repository, Not only that, the temperature is fixed and there are no worries about damp or damage from the elements. There would be nothing worse than digging out Auntie's old will, in which she had left you her jewels, to find that the paper had disintegrated and the lot was now going to the cat's home. No chance of that in the dedicated container. Your inheritance is in safe hands. Care has always been taken of other people's property. It is one of the golden rules of the business. No job was ever too small to be skimped. Delicate porcelain was, at one time, moved in a special contraption called a china van. The floor was removed and the breakables stored below. Furniture was then piled onto the replaced flooring. As well,

Left: *Moving the Sutton Coldfield News in the late 1950s.* **Below:** *Bill Kitchen, seated with his sons Nigel, left and Richard, right, in 1978.* **Bottom:** *The new premises in the 1950s. Originally built on an area of 8,000 sq.ft., nowadays it covers an area of 31,000 sq.ft.*

throughout the 20th century. It is the way that the family business has always operated and intends to do for another 100 years. There have now been five generations of the family involved in the running of the company. After the founder came EJ White, followed by Bill Kitchen and his sons Richard and Nigel. The fifth and, most certainly, not the last are Jamie and Sam. They will be on hand to take the firm into the new millennium. Who knows; perhaps there will be White's vans on a space shuttle to the moon by the end of the next century. So successful have they been that you would not bet against it. What price for a container service to Mars in the following one? Technology has moved us from the horse-drawn dray to the steam-driven vans and right through to transporting across continents. Nothing should be a surprise. It might have been to the driver of the old steam driven vehicle. He had to get up at four o'clock in order to raise enough pressure in the boiler for an eight o'clock start. When people talk about the good old days, remind them of that! Still, they must not have been too bad for White's. It certainly has a rosy future.

White's have handled some of the largest jobs imaginable. In the 1980s, the contents of Aston Hall were removed to store whilst it was being refurbished. Special crates were made. Marble tables, 47 works of art, countless ornaments and all the furniture were taken to headquarters in the high security warehouse.

It has been that reliable and trouble free service that has been the cornerstone of White's business

Top: In 1983 Whites removed and stored the contents of Aston Hall as it underwent refurbishment. Pictured from left to right are Richard Kitchen, Director, John Sugden, Tom Costello, Arthur Smith (retired) and Keith Deeming. **Above left:** *A horse drawn china van taking part in the Birmingham Horse Parade.*

Aston & Fincher Ltd - Riding high on a permanent wave of success

During the 1920s, Galloways Chemists in central Birmingham employed a young dispenser called Mr A E Aston. Mr Aston was an intelligent and astute young man who took a great interest in the various chemists' products, and in 1928 he left Galloways and began manufacturing a range of similar items for sale through chemists, hairdressers and corner shops. Reeves Remedies was one brand and his products soon found favour; lines included eau-de-Colognes, toiletries, a popular ointment for skin disorders called Silvestrine, chemicals for the ladies' trade, and of course that indispensable item for young men-about-town - brilliantine.

Mr Aston added more and more sundry items for hairdressing use to his list, employing up to nine assistants; his wife ran the office. By the second world war he was established as a hairdressers' wholesaler and held accounts with most leading manufacturers of the day. But wartime trading conditions affected his business badly. Controls were imposed on raw materials, with priority given to the war effort; hairdressing products rated low on the list and supplies were severely restricted. Mr Aston had to wind down the business, abandon many of his lines and let his employees go. As a husband and wife team they managed to continue, and played a small but valuable part in keeping up morale by making hair cream which hairdressers bought by the gallon as an alternative to Brylcreme. Because of the shortage of bottles, it left his factory in whatever containers were to hand, and the hairdressers' customers would in turn bring their own empty bottles in for refilling; and so throughout the war Birmingham's own Brylcreme Boys could stay well-groomed. It was after the war that an invention was made which was to revolutionise ladies' hairdressing - cold permanent waving. Characteristically, Mr Aston

immediately set to work and was soon manufacturing his own cold wave; branded ATP, it was among the first cold waves on the market.

Although obtaining raw materials remained a problem to a lesser extent for some years, he was able to begin rebuilding the business and in due course Aston Toilet Products at Dr Johnsons Passage employed a staff of four. By the mid 50s, however, he and his wife had started to lose a little of their youthful energy. Mrs Aston retired in 1957, and Mr Aston decided to continue on just a small scale, working on his own. The couple had no children and the business had been such an important part of Mr Aston's life for 30 years that he was reluctant to give it up, looking upon it as he did as his 'baby', but as he neared 70 he was finding the responsibility increasingly burdensome.

One sunny day in March 1959 he happened to stop for a chat in the street with a casual acquaintance in the same trade. It emerged that Mr Fincher was looking for a fresh opportunity as he felt that his prospects with the company where he worked as a representative were limited. In turn Mr Aston briefly explained his own situation, adding that if he could find someone to buy him out and then employ him, he would. Mr Fincher offered on the spot to do just that, and the two men arranged to meet that weekend to discuss the matter in more detail.

Ideally, what Mr Aston wanted was to hand over the ownership of the business completely and to carry on working there, earning £12 a week; he also wished the business to keep his name. There was also the question

Below: *Delivery vans outside 182 Soho Hill, Handsworth in the early 1970s.*

Left: *W R Fincher presents the Aston & Fincher cup to the winners of a students hairdressing competition at the Birmingham College of Food and Domestic Art in 1970.* **Below:** *The Bristol Cash and Carry.*

customer just starting out in business. No embarrassment ever arose over this as by the time the change of ownership became generally known Aston & Fincher had established excellent credentials of its own.

Not only did Mr Aston bring to the business a vast store of experience and knowledge which proved invaluable in dealings with suppliers, but he was also unfailingly good humoured and a pleasure to work with, and when he died suddenly at the age of 74 he was sadly missed. However, he lived on through his products which Aston & Fincher continued to market, turning ATP cold wave and others into big sellers, produced today by the company in their purpose built manufacturing facility on the Handsworth site.

Victoria Fincher joined her parents and her big brother as soon as she left school, becoming Aston & Fincher's first full-time telephonist, invoice clerk and general office assistant and remaining in post for 20 years. The family team worked extremely hard, determined to prove to the Midlands hairdressing trade that Aston & Fincher could provide the best and most reliable service of any hairdressing wholesaler. Knowing that one of the greatest sources of frustration for a hairdresser was to be told that a particular item which had been ordered specially for a customer's appointment was out of stock, they did their utmost to guarantee complete delivery of every order. Gradually customers came to rely on them; the business grew, more staff were taken on, and before long more space was needed. In August 1963 the company moved to 182 Soho Hill, Handsworth, but expansion continued and it was not until the company moved its current site at 8 Holyhead Road, Handsworth, that the problem of space was finally solved.

of premises, as the lease at Dr Johnsons Passage was not renewable.

Mr Fincher was able to accommodate all Mr Aston's wishes, and by Easter 1959 the deal was finalised. The business would be called Aston & Fincher. Mr Aston had no further stake in it, but was employed at a wage of £12 a week - which made him the highest-paid member of staff. The firm moved into two rooms on the ground floor of a Victorian house at 13 Soho Road, Handsworth, where the rent was £5 a week, and Bob Fincher started the first week's trading on 29th July 1959 with just £211 capital. Apart from Messrs Aston and Fincher themselves, the firm also enjoyed the services of Mrs Fincher and Master Richard Fincher - Richard received a wage of £3 a week, his mother worked unpaid, and Mr Fincher himself took only his expenses at first.

One consequence of Mr Aston's continuing involvement was that the new business could in most cases benefit from the same favourable terms of business which the leading manufacturers had habitually accorded to Mr Aston as a long-term customer with an excellent credit rating who had held accounts with them since before the war. Not realising that the new name signified a complete change of ownership, most companies continued to extend these same privileges, which under normal circumstances they would not have offered to a new

Above: *Family members involved in the firm pictured from right - founder and retired Chairman WR (Bob) Fincher, his son Richard, Managing Director and his grandson Oliver, Sales and Marketing Director.*
Right: *A typical Aston & Fincher 'small town' cash and carry.*

Holyhead Road was destined to make history by becoming the very first cash and carry for the hairdressing trade. Richard and fellow director Len Barber realised that cash and carry, which had been introduced in other trades but never tried in hairdressing, offered a solution to the cash flow problem which often accompanies rapid expansion. Part of the warehouse was refurbished and given a separate entrance. WR (Bob) backed the idea and advertised it in the trade press as 'The Buying Revolution'. It was an immediate success. Hairdressers flocked from all parts of the country to buy in quantity, pay in cash and enjoy the huge cash and carry discounts which Aston & Fincher were able to offer. Soon this revolutionary method of trading had completely eclipsed the old delivery and credit system, and Aston & Fincher's cash

and carry wholesale became known all over the country. By acquiring other wholesalers - sometimes at their own request - and transforming them into thriving firms under the Aston & Fincher banner, they have given hairdressers nationwide easy access to the thousands of necessities - from a hairpin to a complete salon installation - which are always in stock; and whilst competitors have followed suit, Aston & Fincher remain the acknowledged trade leader. Today the company has 26 cash and carrys throughout the country, generating a turnover of some £16 million a year, and with each warehouse carrying thousands of lines the firm truly does supply 'Everything for the hairdresser and beautician'.

So that chance meeting in the street between Mr Aston and Mr Fincher 40 years ago was to have unforseen and far-reaching consequences, resulting as it did in a dramatic change in the distribution chain from manufacturer through wholesaler to retailer in the hairdressing trade in Britain. Meanwhile, Aston & Fincher's success in this sphere has been accompanied by constant product improvement and the introduction of new lines, branded under the highly-respected AF and Hara labels (the Hara hair removing system, for example, is the National brand leader) and exported worldwide.

The company has developed close links with the hairdressing industry over the years. Regular seminars are held to familiarise hairdressers and beauticians with new products and techniques; the company also sponsors hairdressing students at technical colleges and donates cups and shields for competition winners, and participates in the activities of the various trade bodies and charitable organisations.

W R Fincher retired in 1986; Richard then took charge of the company, and his son, the founder's grandson, Oliver joined the staff in 1995, so happily the Fincher family connection is assured. The 40th anniversary of Aston & Fincher was recently celebrated in fine style at Chateau Impney, with every employee invited to share a celebration dinner and stay overnight. The company sets great value on its loyal and hardworking workforce, many of whom have completed 25 years' service, and never underestimates their contribution to the success of the firm. The secret of this success lies in the friendly service and no-gimmick low prices, the wide choice incorporating the firm's own innovative products, and the pleasant surroundings which make a visit to Aston & Fincher's a profitable, interesting, enjoyable and satisfying experience for anyone connected with the hairdressing trade. With 40 years of excellence as Aston & Fincher already to its credit, and a further 31 before that as Aston Toilet Products, the company's aim for the future is simple: to keep on supplying hairdressers and beauticians with the best of everything.

Above: Directors and staff celebrate the 40th anniversary of the firm's founding at Chateau Impney in June 1999. Below: The head office at 8 Holyhead Road, Handsworth.

The family firm where success is always well in hand

Next time you board a bus, coach or train, just notice how comfortable that textured handrail feels in your hand; it was probably made by Gabriel & Company Limited of Birmingham. Gabriel & Company was the first manufacturer to produce textured grip tubing for greater passenger safety, and is the UK's largest manufacturer of handrail systems for the passenger transport vehicle market. It is also one of Birmingham's old-established firms, having been founded in 1884 by Mr Charles Edward Percival Gabriel, known as Percy.

Gabriel & Company today specialises in providing support for travellers, in the literal sense; it could be said that Percy's father 'supported travellers' in a figurative sense - the Reverend John Bath Gabriel was vicar of All Saints, Birmingham. Percy, one of nine children, served an apprenticeship with Messrs Tangyes and went on to work as Manager of the National Arms Factory for a a time. He was also a director of R W Winfield & Company in Cambridge Street; this company, started in 1829 by Robert Walter Winfield, had enjoyed great prestige, exhibiting at the Great Exhibition in London in 1851, but had gone into decline after the death of its founder in 1869. Percy Gabriel, who later became part of the Winfield family through his marriage to Robert Walter Winfield's grand-daughter Emily Snepp in 1888, stepped in and try and save the family business, but eventually, in spite of his efforts, it had to be sold.

In 1884, at the age of 26, Percy Gabriel purchased an existing brass foundry at No. 5 AB Row, at a cost of £235 which included patterns, pattern cards and goodwill, and there, with a workforce of 13, Gabriel & Company came into being.

Left: *Percy Gabriel, founder of the company.*
Below and Bottom: *Some of the moulders and casters who worked for the company.*

Young Percy was full of ideas; the company's printed letter-heads proclaimed Gabriel & Company to be 'Patentees, Mechanical Engineers, Millwrights and Machinists, General Brass Founders and sole Manufacturers of Gabriel's Patent Ball Valve', and early catalogues show a tremendous range of cabinet fittings and general brass castings, such as ornate cast door and drawer handles. Twelve years later Percy expanded, taking over the property next door and purchasing the patterns and tools of another small firm.

The company began to specialise in manufacturing fittings for tramways, buses and railways. Tram fittings offered plenty of scope for Percy Gabriel's active imagination; his catalogue of 'Tramcar, Motor Omnibus and Railway Carriage Handrails and Fittings' listed over 1,700 items. He made anti-rattle door rollers; he made an improved patent spring

button and anti-rattler; he made a patent automatic combined dust-proof anti-rattler and door stop. He also made a patent guard called a 'Save All' to be attached to the front of a tramcar, like a cowcatcher. And in 1914 Percy patented a new aluminium alloy which he had developed. 'Clarus' Metal' contained copper and chromium and purported to be 'as light as aluminium, but stronger than brass'. It was an attractive bright silvery colour, and for many years it was used for all kinds of builders' hardware, including a range of bathroom fittings.

Percy and Emily had two daughters and two sons, and in the same year that Percy patented 'Clarus' Metal' his eldest son Edward made the headlines in an even bigger way. Eleven-year-old Ted was riding his bicycle along Bristol Road when he skidded, ending up on the tram track with a tramcar approaching. The driver spotted him, applied the brakes and brought the tram to a halt 'within its own length'; and by the time the vehicle had stopped, the 'Save All' had safely gathered up boy and bike, and Ted, slightly bruised, was able to climb out and wheel his bike home.

Ted went on to join the business in 1920, and took over after his father's death in 1928. The firm became a limited liability company later that same year, with 'Mr Ted'. as he was called, as Managing Director, and his brother John as Assistant Manager. Their two sisters, Phyllis and Violet, also worked for the firm.

The development of stainless steel provided new opportunities for Gabriel & Company; true to form, it became one of the first firms to manufacture castings in the new material, marketing them under the 'Angel' brand name. A set of early stainless steel control and brake handles produced for the Birmingham Corporation trams has been preserved by the company as a museum piece, having been returned to Gabriel when the trams were scrapped in 1952.

Top: *The workforce in 1914.*
Above left: *The original offices.*

By 1935 Gabriels was established as an important supplier to public transport providers in this country, and also in Africa, India and South America. Over 8,000 different patterns were kept in stock, the workforce had grown to almost 200, and the old factory was becoming distinctly cramped. Edward Gabriel decided to stay on the same site but construct a completely new factory around the old one, bit by bit, so that production could continue. The fine modern structure was almost finished when war broke out in 1939. A temporary wooden facade was erected, and the works turned to the production of armaments including gun mountings, tank track links and electrical fittings for the Admiralty. Work carried on round the clock regardless of power cuts, as the factory had its own power supply and lighting, with two large diesel engines to drive the machines and generators. Output of vital war components was further increased by the acquisition of a small steel foundry on the opposite side of AB Row. Gabriel & Company's works survived intact until July 27th, 1942, when the very last high explosive bomb dropped on Birmingham ripped into the front of the building and destroyed the offices and part of the factory. Another temporary wooden facade was put up, and production was resumed within a couple of weeks.

Top: *The firm supplied handrails to the London Bus Company.* ***Above right:*** *Gabriels handrails and balustrades.*

When peace returned, Gabriel & Company concentrated on finding new applications for stainless steel, making stainless steel castings for the pump and valve industries alongside its extensive range of fittings for the public transport sector. The demand for stainless steel castings increased to such a level that it justified a separate foundry; land adjoining the existing works was purchased and a modern £60,000 factory was built, and opened in 1962. The old aluminium and brass foundries were later closed.

In 1967 Teddy Gabriel died, and leadership of the company passed to his only son Anthony. When the firm celebrated its centenary in 1984, Anthony Gabriel described it as 'a typical Birmingham family business', and paid tribute to 'all the industrious and inventive people' whose hard work had brought success to the company. Although over the years the workforce has grown considerably from the 13 original employees to around 200 at the Abro works today, the family atmosphere and the proud tradition of long-service amongst the workforce has been preserved. In recent year the business has passed from the third generation of the founding family to the fourth; Anthony has been joined by his son, John Edward, managing director at the time of writing. Product development has continued along substantially the same lines, with the introduction in 1992 of architectural applications as an extension of the firm's handrail manufacturing activities.

New 24,000 square foot premises in Hay Hall Road, Tyseley were acquired in November 1996, and Gabriel & Company moved out of the factory in AB Row that had been its home for 112 years. The official opening ceremony was held on

Bottom: *The premises today.*
Below: *Today's management, John and Anthony Gabriel.*

March 25th, 1997. The new £300,000 foundry provided greater capacity and improved facilities; however, by the summer of 98 the factory had been further extended by almost 50 per cent. Nineteen ninety-nine has seen the installation and commissioning of one of the world's most technologically advanced CNC tube bending machines.

Gabriel & Company today remains one of the foremost suppliers of stainless and alloy steel castings to the makers of pumps and valves. Its Architectural Division has completed some very prestigious contracts, including a £500,000 order to supply handrails and balustrading for the impressive new Britannic Assurance headquarters in Wythall, and a £90,000 project to manufacture, supply and fix stainless steel balustrading and balcony rails for a new office block in Colmore Row as part of a renovation project by National Westminster Group Properties. Meanwhile, having been an approved supplier to the railway industry for over 60 years, Gabriel & Company's unrivalled reputation for experience and in-house expertise continues to keep it well ahead of the competition. Recent orders have included a £500,000 contract to supply handrails for buses to be manufactured by the UK's biggest bus builder Water Alexander (Falkirk) Limited for three Far-Eastern bus companies, The Kowloon Motor Bus Company, Hong Kong City Bus Company and the Singapore Bus Company; while another contract in the Far East, a £2.2 million order from GEC-Alsthom Railway Maintenance Services Limited to supply grab rails and partitions for the upgraded rolling stock for the Kowloon-Canton Rail Corporation, represents Gabriel & Company's biggest ever contract to date.

So next time you catch a bus or train, be it in the Far East or Birmingham, take a good look at the handrail. If it's a nice yellow or orange colour, or red, or green, or perhaps blue, with a polyester power coated finish or a 'warm touch' nylon coating, textured with those little diamond-shaped indentations, then it will be part of the Abrobility range; Abrotube is the name of the specially patterned tubular steel which the rails are made from - called Abro after the firm's original home in AB Row. If, on the other hand, you find yourself gripping a plastic rail, then it will most likely be Gabriel's latest product, launched at the 'Coach & Bus 97' Exhibition - a nylon coated handrail designed to provide an even more secure grip for passengers.

So Percy Gabriel's talent for innovation continues, and customers today can benefit from more than a century's experience from a firm which which offers expert technical assistance and helps take the cost out of the products. The company's future is secure; its workforce's jobs are secure; and the man in the street, or rather on the bus, has something safe to hold onto too!

Fittings, as worn by the best furniture

In the Victorian heyday of free enterprise the famous firm of R W Winfield lost the services of two of its experienced employees when George Crofts and George Frederick Assinder left, in 1875, to set up their own firm. The two partners were brothers-in-law, George Crofts having married Lucy Assinder. On deciding to take the step of establishing themselves as brass founders in the 'city of a thousand trades', they set up a brassworks in Lower Essex Street where they began producing the highly-decorative knobs, handles, lion claw casters, door plates, firescreen feet and sundry other ornaments which the Victorians liked to adorn their chests of drawers, tables, doors and windows. Their customers were mainly drawn from the prosperous middle classes - not only local industrialists but also their relatives who had successfully ventured abroad - and the offices of successful business enterprises; in short, all those who liked to, and could afford to, indulge in some show of affluence to please themselves or their friends, or to provide fancy surroundings and an ambience to impress clients in an age with a taste for magnificent clutter.

It was an era of unparalleled expansion for the building and decorative trades. Smart suburbs were being built as fast as the newly-rich could move in, while captains of industry were emulating the aristocracy in building country mansions for themselves. These were sometimes of prefabricated construction with steel girder frames in which great numbers of windows and doors were fitted, all of which would require furnishing with hinges and

Top left: George Crofts, 1840-1926, co-founder of the firm. Above left: George Frederick Assinder, 1850-1926, co-founder of the firm. Right: A very early page of designs for the company's ornate cabinet brassware.

stylish exterior fittings; while inside the house every room would be equipped with the latest styles in furniture and furnishings. Such a market was of course life and breath to Crofts & Assinder. The florid mid-Victorian styles were replaced by the easy natural styles introduced by the pre-Raphaelite movement led by the William Morris coterie.

As the business grew, George Crofts took responsibility for running the factory while Fred Assinder dealt with sales, obtaining lucrative contract work to supply to the spate of hotels, offices and department stores which were appearing all over England in response to demand. After seven years in their first premises, the expanding firm moved to Angelina Street, where it was to remain for almost twenty years before settling at the Standard Brass Works in Lombard Street, its current home. At Angelina Street they continued to design, produce and market their own hand-made products of the highest quality, creating many beautiful hand-chased fittings made from solid brass, until the comfortable Edwardian world was torn apart in 1914. During the Great War the firm, like other similar companies, made war material to government orders, with the emphasis on the strictly utilitarian. When peace returned to a changed world, new fashions replaced the romantic Art Nouveau decor of pre-war years, as the plainer styles of the Art Deco period of the 1930s, and Crofts & Assinder extended its range of styles and finishes accordingly; its aim has always been 'to produce what the best-dressed furniture is wearing'.

During World War Two the company was once again involved in making essential war material, in this case metal casings for radio sets. At first these were provided for ships, aircraft, armoured fighting vehicles and the larger echelons of infantry. At company and platoon level the infantry

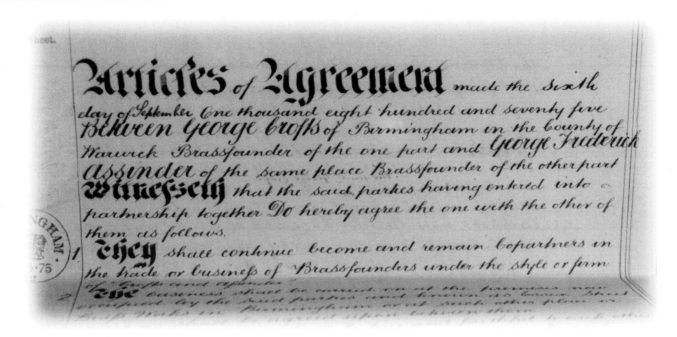

still had to make do with signal flags, pigeons and runners until these were replaced by the heavy back-pack radios which pre-dated the handy little 'walky-talkies' introduced later.

With the declaration of peace, production at Lombard Street gradually reverted to furniture handles and fittings, once more keeping abreast of the latest decorative styles. Over the years the company has consistently maintained its leading place as a supplier of the latest and best to furniture designers and manufacturers through the introduction of new moulds, materials and techniques. More mechanisation has been intro-duced, but the traditional skills have not been lost; some items are still processed and finished by hand today - and the range now includes curtain rails, kitchen and bathroom fittings. The traditional collections of brass fittings remain popular, but a much wider range of materials including zinc, cast iron, ceramics and the woods oak, pine and maple are now also used. Each generation has its own preferences; often, close inspection of an antique chest of drawers reveals the marks where handles have been periodically replaced by successive generations to make it blend in with 'modern' taste in furnishings.

Besides the manufacture of traditional furniture and architectural fittings, in the 1920s, the Company developed an extensive range of

decorative ornamentally embossed furnishing brassware. This became the world famous Lombard Collection which included brass log boxes, firescreens, umbrella stands and waste bins. Over 70 percent of this product was exported worldwide but mostly to North America. The production started in the 1920s ceased on the sale of this side of the business in 1988.

The DIY movement began in the post-war years and slowly developed into the tidal wave of home improve-ments which it is today, allowing many households to benefit from unprecedented levels of luxury in fitted kitchens and elegant bathrooms. Crofts & Assinder contributes to such improvements by supplying handles, knobs and fittings to manufacturers of household furniture and kitchen and bathroom units alike, maintaining those same high standards that prompted a famous New York antique dealer and importer of fine English furniture to

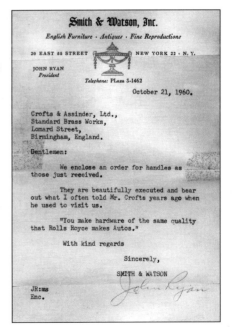

Top: The original Articles of Partnership, 1875.
Above left: One of the company's first business cards.
Right: A testimonial letter from a very satisfied customer in 1960.

write in the 1960s "You make hardware of the same quality that Rolls Royce makes Autos" - high praise indeed! Today's weekend DIY buff can enhance his - or her - furniture by selecting from the innovative designs of exceptional quality available at competitive prices from all good hardware stores, or from Crofts & Assinders' catalogues.

Throughout its history Crofts & Assinder has remained a family firm; it is currently in the hands of the fourth and fifth generations, with chairman Guy Crofts being assisted in the management of the company by his son Richard Crofts. Few companies can have more experience and skill in their chosen sphere of activity. Since 1875 all their pattern designs - some 5,000 to date- have been stored in a pattern room situated in what is referred to as 'the company dungeon', and in recent years many of these designs have been re-issued. Customers are cordially invited to visit the old pattern room, where they can select designs from the original patterns which Crofts & Assinder will then reproduce for them, either by traditional sand-casting methods or, for larger volumes, as hot stampings or zinc diecastings. To this end the Company took a 50 percent interest in a contract high pressure diecasting business in order to safeguard supplies of handle castings. This company has now expanded as a major supplier to many other diverse trades and has recently moved into new premises.

The company can also produce original designs to a customer's own specifications, no matter how unusual the request. So, whatever the age of the furniture, the period of the room and the decor chosen by the home owner, Crofts & Assinder can provide just the right finishing touches in the shape of stylish handles and fittings - whether it be a design from its current extensive range of products which encompasses both antique and contemporary styles, a design from bygone years chosen from its pattern room, or a design created specially for the occasion. For more than one hundred years homes have been enhanced by Crofts & Assinder's stylish, high-quality, well-designed hardware. No doubt the homes of the next millennium will continue in the same fine tradition with the Crofts family assisted by the management team led by Caron Tromans.

Top left: *Percy Crofts, 1872-1952.* **Left:** *An ornate door handle.* **Above:** *Ronald Crofts, 1907-1985.* **Below:** *Guy Crofts, Chairman of the company.*

The icing on the cake

'You get better cakes than this at Drucker's,' the British tourist complained in a loud voice.

The holidaymaker sitting at the next table in the pleasant Austrian cafe smiled, but kept her thoughts to herself. How could the dissatisfied customer nearby

know that her poor opinion of the pastry she was eating had been overheard by a member of Drucker's staff?

The tourist's reaction was understandable; Drucker's gateaux and pastries had been regarded as second to none since the patisserie opened in the mid 1960s.

It was 1939 when, under the menacing cloud of Nazi persecution, Andre Drucker hastily left his home in Prague and fled to Britain. A textile designer by profession, he had to take what jobs he could, painting posters for cinemas, working as a commercial artist, and even delivering milk for the Co-op. He settled in Birmingham, where he met and married his wife, Gretl.

Andre Drucker's sights were set far higher than drifting from one dead-end job to another, however, and in 1958, with a loan of £1,000 he acquired the site of an old book shop in Aston Street, Gosta Green, and opened a continental coffee lounge, La Boheme. Coffee bars were by the late 1950s establishing themselves on every high street across the country, their juke boxes churning out 'The Purple People Eater' and 'The Chipmunk Song' as well as the latest offering from 'Elvis the Pelvis'. But Mr Drucker had in mind the kind of client who preferred Puccini to Presley; he bought a piano and a radiogram, and classical music and well-known cabaret melodies played discreetly in the background of the coffee lounge. With artistic flair he decorated the walls of La Boheme with his own paintings, and created an art gallery on the first floor of the building. And the enterprising Mr Drucker gave his customers other reasons to stay awhile and drink coffee, providing them with newspapers and even a chess board.

La Boheme, he felt, lacked only one thing - the ability to offer its customers a selection of superior quality cakes. It was time, Mr Drucker decided, that Birmingham had a high class coffee and cake shop like the ones that were commonly seen on the Continent. When a small shop in Moseley fell vacant he converted the rear into a bakery and equipped the front room with three tables, a counter and a refrigerated display. He appointed a master baker from Germany, agreed the patisserie range, and Drucker's Vienna Patisserie was up and running. Business remained slow, however, until Birmingham's rather conservative customers grew used to the unfamiliar and rather exotic confectionery that were served at Drucker's.

For the Drucker family, the involvement with La Boheme and the new Vienna Patisserie often meant working six or even seven days a week; working alongside Mr Drucker in the shop and the bakery were his wife and their son Stephen. In 1968 Stephen Drucker took over the running of the company.

Left: *The founder behind the counter in La Boheme in 1958.* **Below:** *A picture of the original premises La Boheme in 1958.*

fell vacant, they were taken over one by one until eventually the entire building was acquired.

Mike Baker, Joint Chairman with Stephen Drucker, joined the company in 1978. They had first met at the tender age of eleven at King Edward's Five Ways School after which Mike went to work for some ten years with multinational companies in North America, reaching the position of Vice President for the Seven Up Company before returning home and teaming up with Stephen. The two old friends have driven the company forward together and, remarkably, with never a cross word.

Above: *Stephen Drucker pictured in the bakery which opened in 1973.*

Eventually, a second and then a third shop was opened, and the firm began to handle a certain amount of wholesale business. Growth of the retail business continued, but was hampered by the considerable cost of high street locations, the need for fresh patisserie every day, and by a lack of workers who were skilled in creating the distinctive confections that had already marked Drucker's out as second to none in the field. The fact that the patisserie is hand-finished still distinguishes their creations, and Strawberry St Honoré and Grand Marnier Gateaux continue to delight the palates of customers across the country. The Grand Marnier, in fact, won both Dessert Product and Product of the Year at the prestigious British Frozen Food Federation's annual awards in 1996.

By the early 1970s business was outstripping the small bakery in Moseley, and in 1973 Drucker's moved their production to a former printing works a mile or so away. It was an appropriate move - the German word for printer is 'Drucker'! Producing for both retail and wholesale at the same time, however, was becoming a pressure, and it was decided that the two sides of the business should be run separately. The frozen foods division was transferred to an empty unit at Sarehole Road in Hall Green, where a skilled team known as the Sugar and Spice Girls still produce cakes and gateaux for wholesale distribution. As more units in the building

As the company expanded, the operations were split into three divisions, each of which had its own manufacturing facility. Further growth in the retail side of the business resulted in a total of 23 shops trading as Drucker's Vienna Patisserie, including a joint venture with Thorntons of 'Chocolate Heaven' fame at The Fort Shopping Park.

Other new developments involved the installation of new technology and information systems. Where Andre Drucker made do with a small oven, a mixer, a gas ring and that essential piece of culinary equipment - a rolling pin - Drucker's staff can today work with automatic pastry rollers, walk-in fridges and freezers, twelve large rotary ovens and a forty foot long chiller tunnel. And how many customers are aware that the company has its own strawberry fields in Huelva in Southern Spain? An incredible 25 tonnes of fresh strawberries go into such seasonal favourites as strawberry flans and strawberry tartlets.

Today Drucker's high quality patisserie enjoys countrywide fame, their frozen products going into hotels, restaurants, ferries and airlines, while since 1996 customers shopping at supermarket giants Tesco can enjoy a whole range of Drucker's chilled confections. This particular contract hung in the balance at one stage, when ten months into production fire swept through the bakery producing the chilled cakes for Tesco. Drucker's were swift to react, and within six

additions to the already extensive range of frozen foodservice products and super-market products.

And what of the future?

More of the same, naturally. But that does not signify that the go-ahead company are content to sit back and enjoy the success they have worked towards for the last 40 years! Plans for future development are already in place, and the firm hopes to eventually see the setting up of an export division. After all, what could possibly be more fitting than one day seeing Drucker's patisserie on sale in Vienna? That would be truly the 'icing on the cake'!

weeks of the fire they were back in production in temporary buildings. In September 1998 production began again in new and larger premises.

The 'secret ingredient' that has contributed so much to the company's many achievements is put down to the quality of their staff, who are committed to providing their customers with the highest quality product served in a professional and friendly manner. A vital part of the day to day running of the firm is the systematic training programme that gives the workforce the opportunity to develop their own skills and potential.

Another important part of Drucker's presence in Birmingham lies in its support for local charities such as Walsgrave Hospital's Cancer Ward Appeal, and their sponsorship of various musical events that are staged in the city. The regular New Year's Day concerts at Symphony Hall are sponsored by Drucker's, who specially make and pack a total of 4,500 cakes to present to members of the audience.

The company continues to develop, and recent expansion has seen the estab-lishing of a brand new production unit at Granby Avenue, new shops in Worcester and Cheltenham - warmly welcomed by the locals - and further

Above left: The copy of Edouard Manet's famous painting, "A bar at the Folies-Bergère" used behind most Drucker's counters with cakes substi-tuted for the wine and Mr Drucker and Mr Baker in the background.
Left: Stephen Drucker and Mike Baker, joint Chairmen. *Below:* A Viennese concert at the Old Town Hall, one of many musical events sponsored by Druckers.

The learning community for girls which is almost 125 years old and still going strong!

Education for girls was the subject of much discussion in the 18th and early 19th centuries, but the quaint notion that girls should be treated as the intellectual equal of boys was largely dismissed. Well brought up young ladies were to be admired for their 'accomplishments', not for their cleverness. The daughter of a reasonably wealthy family might attend one of the tiny, private girls' boarding schools which existed, but she would be more likely to have a governess who would teach her what she needed to know, including embroidery, nature study, art, music and a little French. This was considered sufficient to equip her for her future role as a wife and mother. However, by the mid-19th century characters like Miss Buss and Miss Beale had begun to express radical views on the subject, and

parents began to think more carefully about their daughters' education. All over the country, new schools were being founded to prepare girls for the same examinations as boys; and in December 1875 Edgbaston manufacturer George Dixon sent a circular to 52 leading local families, inviting them to attend a meeting to discuss the 'propriety of establishing a HIGH SCHOOL FOR GIRLS in Edgbaston'.

At this meeting it was proposed to set up a modern, independent, non-

Top right: *A hockey team in the 1890s.*
Above: *Miss Cooper and her staff.*
Right: *The front of the school in 1951.*

sectarian girls' day school. Distinguished local families from both Quaker and Unitarian backgrounds, including the Albrights, Beales, Crosskeys, Chamberlains, Dales, Dawsons, Frys, Kenricks, Lloyds, Martineaus, Sturges and Wilsons, agreed with the proposals and joined together to support the founding of Edgbaston High School.

The school's first premises were at 284 Hagley Road, on the corner of Harborne Road (now the site of the Swallow Hotel). Miss Alice Jane Cooper was appointed the School's first Headmistress, a post she was to hold until 1895. The School opened in 1876, following an entrance examination in which 76 girls were successful. Very soon it became necessary to extend the building; by 1878 the School had doubled in size, and to accommodate it The Laurels, at 280 Hagley Road, was purchased.

Under Miss Cooper, the school was quick to attain high academic standards. Examination successes were impressive; by 1881 one girl had won a scholarship to Oxford, and before long many 'old girls' had gone on to obtain Oxbridge degrees. Miss Cooper was also a keen advocate of extra-curricular activities; various clubs and societies were set up, and the girls' enthusiastic participation in cricket matches raised a few eyebrows. A school magazine was launched, entitled "Laurel Leaves" (after The Laurels), and this gives a charming insight into the lively and stimulating

fully-heated indoor swimming pool. Recent additions include a new Art Block built in 1985, a new Music School added in 1992, and a new wing with a large IT Centre, new laboratories and an updated and enlarged Home Economics Department, which was opened in 1994.

Edgbaston High School, with its excellent, modern facilities, continues to build on the traditions of its founders, seeking to foster breadth of educational opportunity based on the academic curriculum at the heart of the school, and to ensure that all its pupils benefit from this. EHS is one of the country's leading girls' independent schools, and is the only school of this size in Birmingham to offer continuity of education to girls only, between the age of two-and-three-quarters and 18. It is a caring, lively School which reflects the multi-cultural life of

environment which existed at Edgbaston High School even in those early days.

Following Miss Cooper's retirement Miss Eliza Japp became Headmistress, and she introduced hockey, medical inspection, uniforms and the boarding house before resigning in 1899 to marry, and return to her native Scotland. Her successor was Miss Tarleton Young, who was responsible for the addition of the gymnasium and the Preparatory School before leaving in 1924; subsequent headmistresses have included Miss Winifred Casswell, who guided the School through the difficult years of the second world war, and Miss Edith Hopkins whose boundless energy proved invaluable when in 1963 the School, numbering some 860 pupils, moved to its current site on Westbourne Road.

Today, this 14-acre site offers excellent facilities which are constantly refurbished and updated on a 'rolling programme'. The Pre-Preparatory Department, the Preparatory Department and the Senior School each has its own separate, purpose-built accommodation. There are three hockey pitches, an athletics track, 12 all-weather tennis courts and a

Birmingham and where a strong sense of community and involvement is paramount. The girls receive a stimulating and challenging education which leads them to exceed expectations more frequently than simply match them; and former pupils of Edgbaston High School will happily testify to the School's success in building confidence in its girls, developing good communications skills and sending out lively young women equipped to make a valuable all-round contribution to society.

Top left: The Laurels Gym in 1957. Above: Miss Wallis teaching History to Upper Fourth, 1975. Right: Miss Elizabeth Mullenger, Headmistress of Edgbaston High School for Girls since January 1998.

Where promotion is all in a day's work

Buckingham Street, Hockley has been the home of A J Gilbert for almost 90 years. Today, the firm occupies a much larger site, where the engineering factory shares its offices with its close relative and neighbour, Executive Promotions Limited. But while the place remains the same, the output of the factory has become undeniably more sophisticated over the years. When the original factory was opened on this site by Mr A J Gilbert in 1915 it was equipped simply with hand presses, which were used to manufacture metal labels from brass, steel and tin. The business continued along these lines for a number of years, first under the ownership of Mr Gilbert, who converted it to a limited company in 1920, and subsequently run by brothers Horace and Herbert Burns who purchased the business from its founder.

During the second world war Gilbert's factory, like many others, was taken over for the fulfilment of Ministry of Defence orders, and it is in the years since the war that the company has developed into the market where it has established its niche - promotional giftware.

As Birmingham's comprehensive rebuilding programme got underway, Gilberts was very fortunate in being able to acquire the site adjoining its existing factory. This made it possible for the rebuilding work to be carried out and the move into the new premises accomplished with a minimum of disruption. Since then the firm has also acquired the building next to its new site, giving it a total area of 32,000 square feet.

The factory still uses hand presses, but these are today used in conjunction with other machinery such as power presses, friction screw presses, hi-ton presses, HME knuckle presses, sewing machines, polishing lathes, and resin applicators. There is also a fully-equipped tool and die department. Next door, the design team of Executive Promotions Limited works with the marketing department to develop customers'

Top right: *Herbert Burns and his Accountant in 1952.* **Left:** *The workshop pictured in the 1950s.* **Below:** *The original company premises on Buckingham Street.*

the back, and when lost keys are returned to the company, it is able to locate the owner of the key-ring from its records. The company regards this facility as just another part of the service it provides to its customers.

With a client base spanning a wide spectrum of commerce and industry - breweries, finance houses, garages and giant corporations - the design team have plenty of scope to exercise their strong creative talents on an extremely diverse range of products. The success of the company is a tribute to the its forward-looking attitude, and by seizing its opportunity to expand and diversify from its traditional product range into the needs of today's promotional gift industry, it has secured a place for British-made goods at the forefront of this competitive industry.

own designs into promotional items which will be put into production in Gilbert's factory - products from parasols to paperknives, briefcases to bottletops, key fobs to coasters or even a canteen of cutlery. Items can be finished in almost any available finish; the factory employs modern production techniques to create a novel and attractive range of promotional gifts with great impact. The skill and expertise of the staff, combined with the advantages of in-house manufacture, means that customers receive a much better deal than they would elsewhere. Production facilities are geared towards offering total flexibility, and millions of pieces are produced each year. All types of metals are used, but items made from leather and other materials can also be supplied, and the company's own range of goods is complemented by a small selection of imported products to provide customers with a complete, across-the-range service.

Over the years the firm has been involved in a variety of highly original and eye-catching promotions, but one of its more innovative diversifications must be the Nautical Heritage side of the business. This venture came into being when the company was offered an opportunity to make memorabilia from part of the propellor from the Queen Mary and the main foremast of the Cutty Sark.

Another subsidiary, which arose out of manufacturing key-rings, is Executive Key Recovery Limited, a company which specialises in recovering lost keys. Each key-ring has a serial number and a return address on

A J Gilbert has remained in the hands of the Burns family, having passed from Horace and Herbert to Horace's son Tony, who has now been joined by his own son Nathan Burns. Tony and Nathan, together with Lucy Cooper who assists in running the company, put in a regular appearance at the annual International Spring Fair at the NEC, where visitors to the the the A J Gilbert stand can admire a selection of colourful and inspirational items from this innovative company's extensive and appealing range of promotional gifts and incentives.

Top left: A promotions stand in 1997.
Above left: The current company premises.
Below: An aerial view of the company premises, 1997.

Where success is much more than just pot luck

Buncher & Haseler Limited admits to being 150 years old in 1999, although John Haseler is known to have been making jewellery in Branston Street, in the heart of Birmingham's Jewellery Quarter, as far back as 1826. John Haseler was succeeded by son Edward, who had trained as a die-sinker; Edward Madeley Haseler went into partnership with William Buncher in 1849, and thus Buncher & Haseler was formed.

For 50 years Buncher & Haseler carried on making gold and silver jewellery, officially classing themselves as jewellers stampers and die-sinkers, but at the turn of the century the firm branched out into manufacturing metal photograph frames, which were very popular at this period. The

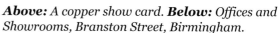

business had by this time passed to William Buncher's son Harold, and Robert Christopher Rodgers who was Edward Haseler's son-in-law. For the next decade or so they manufactured a varied range of photo frames together with other fancy goods and advertising novelties, such as trinket boxes, ash trays, match-boxes, paper knives and a tremendous variety of calendars, all in metal; when German-made cigarette cases came onto the market in this country a whole new section was added to Buncher & Haseler's factory to mass-produce nickel-plated cigarette cases, which were sold at 33s a gross (£1.51 for twelve dozen, in today's currency). Buncher and Haseler was one of the

Above: *A copper show card.* ***Below:*** *Offices and Showrooms, Branston Street, Birmingham.*

first manufacturers to use aluminium. Aluminium was at first very expensive, and in 1912 the firm made an initial purchase of a few hundredweights at a cost which is not recorded but which is likely to have been higher in pounds sterling, let alone in value, than it would be today. The company then embarked on manufacturing the Longlife kettles, teapots, colanders, straight and bellied stewpans and all the other items of kitchenware for which it has been famous ever since.

The British housewife was not won over to aluminium cooking utensils overnight. Considerable efforts had to be made by the industry, and Buncher & Haseler put out a wonderful little promotional booklet, 'dedicated to the busy housewife'. This booklet begins by explaining that aluminium cooking utensils rank amongst inventions such as the vacuum cleaner and the electric iron which make a woman's household chores not only easier but *interesting*. It then goes on to explain what aluminium is and emphasise reassuringly that many foods contain alumina and fresh eggs in particular contain quite a lot, before extolling the advantages of aluminium over iron and enamel: not only does it not rust or chip, it is more economical (because it is a better conductor of heat), and, most important of all from a woman's point of view, it is shinier - after all, 'What woman does not experience a feeling of pride from her shelf of silvery saucepans?' A note of caution is added. Only quality products like Longlife guarantee lifelong service and satisfaction ('the first cost is the last'); the housewife must not be tempted to buy

cheap aluminiumware which will not give good service, even though the initial outlay appears lower. In other words, she should avoid what, in those liberated days before political correctness, the company's advertising department had no qualms in calling 'foreign rubbish' - a term unlikely to be sanctioned by current sales and marketing manager Richard Barrett!

Thanks to (or perhaps in spite of) such persuasive marketing, and no doubt also due to the undoubted advantages of aluminium combined with subsequent reductions in price, the demand for aluminium cooking utensils has grown immeasurably, and Buncher & Haseler now stand at the forefront of the thriving aluminium holloware manufacturing industry. Longlife, first made in 1912, remains one of the best-respected trademarks in the catering trade; the firm's catering sundries are made under the tradename of Caterlife, while its range of items for the bar and cellar trade are marketed under the name of Thorben. The company has developed a highly efficient distribution system, selling through the network of distributors which supplies the catering and bar trades and exports to Europe, the Middle East and Africa. As well as manufacturing the widest possible range of aluminiumware, Buncher & Haseler also continues to offer metal spinning and presswork subcontracting services to clients from many sectors of industry.

Buncher & Haseler is today a privately-owned Limited Company with an annual turnover of over £4million, a figure which, due in no small part to the efforts of directors Roger Brain and Shirley Dodd, is double that of four years ago. The firm still occupies the Branston Street premises which have been its home for a century and a half, and now also has a second factory nearby. With an experienced workforce of around 90 and the latest state-of-the-art machinery, Buncher & Haseler, just like its products, is guaranteed a bright future.

Above: A small advertising magazine in 1911.
Left: Stainless steel pots and pans of the 90s.

At the cutting edge of technology

Burcas began life as a factoring company during the second world war, and spent its first decade, between 1941 and 1951, distributing files, drills, reamers and miscellaneous small tools to large firms involved in the war effort. Its founders were Messrs Burrows and Castle, hence the name Burcas, and its first home was an office in Birmingham. The involvement of the Castle family was short-lived, and before long it was being run by two Messrs Burrows: Sydney, the original Mr Burrows, and his nephew Reginald. The business expanded and moved to new premises, and in 1951 a factory was set up on another site and the manufacturing operations of Burcas began, specialising in metal cutting form tools for some of the major engineering companies who were operating in Birmingham at that time - BSA, Morris Motors and Morris Commercial.

Manufacturing and distribution continued in separate premises until 1956, when both sides of the business were moved into Paragon Works at Hockley Hill. Unfortunately, before the end of the decade plans for the Paragon Flyover were threatening to put an end to the Paragon Works, and the premature deaths of both Sydney

and Reginald Burrows brought further upset to the business. Mr Jack Burrows, who inherited the company, decided to set up a brand new factory, and as a result the entire operation moved to its present location at Park Lane, Handsworth, Birmingham. During the 1960s Jack Burrows, assisted by Works Director Mr Elwood Deakin, expanded the manufacturing facilities at Handworth by investing in conventional machine tools such as centre lathes, millers and grinders, as well as a considerable range of inspection equipment. In addition a second factory was set up at College Road, Perry Barr, where punches and dies for cold forging and the fastener industry were manufactured, as were work rest blades and wear parts for the automotive industry.

The company continued to focus on manufacturing throughout the 1970s, establishing itself in the market place as a specialist manufacturer and allowing the distributive side of the business to decline. However, it became necessary to find ways of cutting back when the industry was faced with a recession in 1980, and Burcas' solution was to bring all its manufacturing facilities under one roof to reduce overheads. The Perry Barr site was vacated, and workshops and offices were condensed into the 1,250 square metres of space available at the company's buildings in Park Lane. The company was headed at this time by Mr Michael Burrows, and with the assistance of his new Works Director, Mr Bryan Hipkiss,

Top left: *Michael Burrows.* ***Below:*** *Precision grinding in the late 1950s.*

from Magneti Marelli (formerly Lucas). All the redundant toolmakers from Magneti Marelli were offered full time employment with Burcas ensuring the standard of supply. The last decade has seen considerable expansion. This has been effected both through acquisition, with the purchase of Ian P Banks in 1993 and Aldridge Tool in 1998, and through growth; the company has expanded into the adjoining premises at Park Lane and now also has a factory and workshop at Smethwick. Other new initiatives include a computerised manufacturing information system introduced in 1998 and a recent comprehensive skills flexibility training programme; the company achieved BS EN ISO 9002 registration in May 1992 and is currently working towards the Investors in People award. With its forward-looking approach and a much wider and varied range of products than 50 years ago, the company has never lost sight of its beginnings and remains essentially a family venture devoted to providing a product of exceptional quality and reliability at a competitive cost - a formula which will be the basis of the business for the next 50 years.

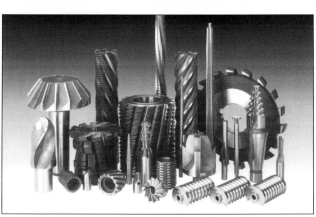

Top left: *Engineering in the 1960s.*
Above left: *Precision Cutting Tools.* **Below:** *One of the new state-of-the-art precision hard turning machines Burcas has recently invested in, keeping the company at the forefront of technology and ensuring its future success.*

he set about restructuring the business. A new venture introduced at this time was the manufacture of special knives and guillotines for the paper and printing industry; since this diversification began in 1981 it has proved extremely successful, and today these products, manufactured from high-alloy steels and tungsten carbide and sold direct to the end user, account for 31 per cent of Burcas' overall turnover.

Another very significant part of the company's business today is its Service Division, and this was started in October 1989, following the appointment of Mr Dale Chambers, an experienced service engineer. Expansion of this division led to Burcas winning the service contract for Stenhoj in 1991, and this in turn led to the company being awarded UK agency for the comprehensive range of Stenhoj hydraulic presses later that same year. A new factory site in Smethwick was opened to accommodate this section and also the Press Tool workshop that Burcas took on in 1993

Efficient service tempered with dignity

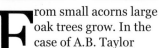

From small acorns large oak trees grow. In the case of A.B. Taylor Funeral Services Ltd, this was especially true in the early days. It was from solid timbers of elm and oak that the first coffins were constructed. The family business has been in Quinton for over 70 years, operating from two different sites. It was in 1927, about 400 yards from its current position, that Augustus Bernard Taylor and his wife, Emma Daisy, opened their premises for the first time. Gus, as he was known to all who knew him, had a firm grounding in the trade. He had been apprenticed to a company of funeral directors and, as an excellent craftsman, soon became a well respected coffin maker. Back in those days, just after World War I, the company often received telegrams informing it of a bereavement. A pony and trap would be hired and a coffin duly despatched to the home of the deceased. Those were the days when loved ones would often be laid out in the best room and friends and family

came to view the departed for a final time. With his beloved Daisy, Gus branched out in a small way at a most difficult time. The years of the depression were upon them and it was a time to tighten belts. However, this did not stop the firm from sticking to its beliefs in the level of quality service provided. Perhaps it was the determination born of those hard times that helped give Taylor's the belief that anything rightly done, however humble, was something that was noble and to be cherished. Not surprisingly, the company continues to hold to that view. It is recognised that the people who are coming to A.B. Taylor are doing so at the saddest period of their lives. They need efficient service, tempered with dignity. This is supplied by a business with a friendly and understanding face. The personal touch is obvious and gratefully received.

Nowadays, Taylor's has grown into a funeral director service on a more diverse scale than in the past. There is also a huge demand for their Rolls-Royce wedding cars. A fleet of gleaming cars sits proudly on the forecourt waiting to whisk some blushing bride off to the altar. The limousines have served this purpose for three generations. However, the brides and the cars have changed. Neither of them is the original! At one time, the private hire side of the business used to see sales reps being carried on visits to their customers, babies off to be christened and ladies to tea parties and coffee

Above, both pictures: *The founder Augustus Bernard Taylor and his wife Emma Daisy.*
Below: *The original premises.*

mornings. Although the cars are now also used on more grand occasions, such as TV, film and promotional work, A.B. Taylor's still prides itself in offering quality and choice at a reasonable cost.

A year after Augustus Taylor died, A.B. Taylor Funeral Services became a limited company in 1959, something that would have been hard to imagine in those first few years on Hagley Road West. It was to that semi-rural surrounding that Gus and Daisy brought their three children, Bernard, Cecilia and Kenneth, for their first steps along the road of their adventure. Sadly, Kenneth was to die from leukaemia at the tender age of 18. On a happier note, a fourth child, Philip, came along in 1925. It was he, supported by his wife, Bess, who worked many a long hour and weekend, ensuring that the business grew on the sound foundation provided by his parents. Their children, Susan, Nicholas and Andrew, have grown up in a world of smooth and polished veneers and shiny coachwork. Under Philip's guidance, as he is still highly committed to the company and working with an interest that he has never lost, A.B. Taylor continues to flourish and expand. It has not been all plain sailing. In the 30s the family home and

business premises were compulsorily purchased under a road widening scheme on Hagley Road West. It was decided to relocate to Wolverhampton Road South, where it remains to-day. The original premises were on a main road site and the enforced move was to have been onto and excellent business site on a new dual carriageway. It was a struggle financially but prospects were good. However the best laid plans of mice and men etc. By now, 1937 there was a war looming and road building was stopped. So where there should have been a new road was a small-holding with chickens and pigs! For the next 30 years Gus Taylor worked in a cul-de-sac and the road was finally opened in the 1960s! However, so high was the reputation and so hard did he and Philip work, that the firm grew into one as solid as those oak timbers they used to use.

Top: The new premises on Wolverhampton Road South shortly after the firm moved there.
Above left: *The premises today with funeral and wedding cars on the forecourt.* ***Below:*** *The Taylor family with some of their cars.*

A College of distinction

Above: The 60s building site from which emerged a Queen's Anniversary Prize-winning college.

Being singled out by the recommendation of Egon Ronay as well as having a number of awards tucked under its belt is no mean achievement for a College that started life in the late 19th century as the Municipal Technical School. Back then the school offered simple courses in cookery and household science. Described by TV celebrity chef Gary Rhodes in a recent interview as 'The best catering College in the country', the Birmingham College of Food, Tourism and Creative Studies has travelled a long and exciting road since its humble beginnings!

The Technical School grew and developed under a number of different names and, one by one, new departments were added and separate buildings came into use. It was 1968 when the current premises in Summer Row were officially opened by the Duke of Edinburgh. In the late 1980s came further changes, and the College emerged with the name it bears today and with a far wider programme of courses. Eventually control of the College passed from Birmingham City Council to the College Corporation.

With the newly established independence came various opportunities, including an increase in funding, a selection of new courses, and the freedom to offer places to a greater number of students. The College has achieved well-deserved success in many different ways. Finance is one area that has become a recognised headache in the field of further education, but the Birmingham College of Food became the most finan-

cially viable institution in the Country. The levels of student achievement at the College are exceptionally high and in 1996 the College achieved the best grades awarded in a national inspection carried out by the Further Education Funding Council. Further awards began to come their way, with the Charter Mark recognising the high quality of their service delivery in 1996, and the same year the recognition of the College's positive approach to work with disabled people. They achieved the Investors in People Award, which recognises the quality of staff training and development, the following year. In 1998 the College was awarded the prestigious Queen's Anniversary Prize for Higher and Further Education.

The courses offered by the College cover an exciting range of subjects: hotel, tourism and leisure management, consumer management, caring, food, hairdressing, beauty therapy, salon management and the culinary arts, with appropriate qualifications that extend from NVQs to degree and postgraduate courses. The salons operate on a commercial basis and are open to the public, offering a range of beauty therapy treatments and hair styling.

The College boasts four training restaurants - three of which are open to the public. They are considered by many to be some of the best places to eat in the

which they find invaluable when moving into their careers. In addition, European and international links have been set up to enable students to travel and gain work experience in other parts of the world.

The needs of the students, the programme content, the opportunities for career development and further study, are of paramount importance to

Midlands. Quite literally, there is something for everyone, whether the customer wants to dine out in style or is looking for a quick pub snack. The College's appropriately named Cap and Gown tavern pub has bar snacks ranging from the famous Birmingham Balti to king prawns and oyster sauce with Chinese greens. The Brasserie restaurant - recommended in Egon Ronay's Britvic Guide - offers a versatile range of starters, light meals and salads, with choice dishes such as deep fried crab cakes and smoked duck breast featuring on the menu. Diners searching for a sophisticated setting for a mouth-watering celebration meal can find that elusive touch of luxury at the Atrium restaurant, where the food and service are unsurpassed.

The Brasserie has been at the forefront in providing experience and scope for the talents of students preparing to take up hotel and restaurant management. They organise regular theme nights at the Brasserie, from 'the swinging 60s' to the gun totin' Wild West. Live music, a plentiful supply of liquid refreshment and a menu designed in keeping with the theme of the evening all play their part in making theme nights fun for everyone.

What sets the Birmingham College of Food, Tourism and Creative Studies apart is their involvement with the cultural and commercial life of the city, which offers the students first-hand experience in dealing with the real face of the public - experience

the College which was described in the Queen's Anniversary Award of 1998 as a 'centre of excellence'. The Principal and his staff make that their continued aim - both now and into the next millennium.

Above Left: Students creating mouthwatering dishes in the College's superb kitchens.
Top right: All of the College's degree and postgraduate programmes are awarded by the University of Birmingham.
Below: The college's impressive entrance was built in 1997.

When you need someone to act on your behalf - ask Shakespeare!

The sight of a firm of solicitors called Shakespeares in Bennetts Hill, Birmingham, may well conjure up images of quill pens, copperplate script and dramatic deeds in the minds of passers-by; and this may not be so very inappropriate, because although today the practice has a reputation for its forward-looking approach, the history of the firm can be traced back for well over 150 years.

As is the case for most long-established legal firms, the present practice of Shakespeares, staffed by around 160 personnel offering between them a comprehensive range of specialisms, has evolved through a succession of partnerships, amalgamations and associations. Henry Plunkett, who began practising as long ago as 1856, became part of the partnership of Plunkett & Shakespeare in 1861; known briefly as Shakespeare & Co, this firm in 1896 became Shakespeare & Vernon, a name which it was to retain for 90 years, until the formation of Shakespeare Duggan Lea & Co in 1986.

The firm of Duggan Lea & Co with which Shakespeare merged can itself be traced back through various branches. Duggan & Elton was established in 1902 and subsequently joined with the long-established practice of Ansell & Sherwin, founded by Joseph Ansell in 1863, to form Duggans in 1970. Duggans was incorporated in Duggan Lea & Co in 1974, along with Freeman Cross & Pitt and Harold Roberts & Lea. The survival of this latter practice was due to a large extent to Harold

Roberts' persistence in overcoming the many problems he had to face, the first of which was his own ill-health. Harold Roberts was born in 1884 and died in 1950. As a young man he was very deaf and prone to sickness; he was educated by private tutors at his home in Bridgewater, Somerset, and entered the legal profession at 16, serving his articles until he was 21, which was the lowest possible age for a solicitor to be admitted. He then spent some time in the USA before becoming a Managing Clerk for a firm at Moorgate in the City of London. Nine months later the firm which employed him went bankrupt. His next appointment was in Leicester, with a firm called Hinks, who had placed an advertisement in the Law Society's Gazette. While in Leicester he married, and as his prospects in Leicester were limited he moved to Birmingham, where he bought a run-down practice with the intention of building it up. The war intervened, however; Harold wanted to go into the Navy but his state of health was considered too poor, so he served in RNAS and spent some months quarantined at Crystal Palace as a carrier of spotted fever. He survived the war, but his practice did not, so he had to start again. This time he fared better. He entered public life, becoming Councillor for Soho Ward from 1921 and going on to be elected Lord Mayor in 1936;

Above: *Alderman Harold Roberts MP, whose own practice, Harold Roberts & Lea merged with Duggans in 1974.*

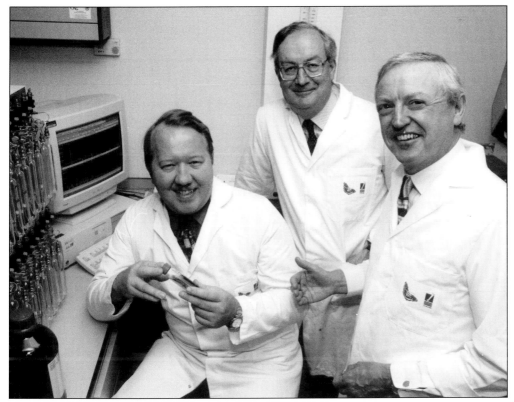

experience and experience, which it has adapted to meet present-day client needs. Offering specialist advice and assistance to institutions and businesses, charities and individuals, Shakespeares excels in finding practical solutions to suit every individual situation, and tries to avoid jargon, communicating in plain English whether it is dealing with corporate finance and commercial property transactions or probate, marital disputes or debt recovery, intellectual property infringement or medical negligence, trusts or fraud. Operating a structure designed to make its full range of expertise available to all clients while building up an in-depth understanding of their individual needs, the firm remains committed to moving forward as it continues to adapt to meet clients' changing needs and expectations.

from the early 1920s onwards his firm prospered, and he was eventually able to leave a thriving practice, which after his death in 1950 continued as Harold Roberts & Lea until 1974, when it became part of Duggan Lea & Co.

The practice became known as Shakespeares in 1990, and since that time it has amalgamated with a number of other firms including Bettinsons and F H Pepper & Tangye, established in 1893 and 1891 respectively. Bettinsons remained a family firm for three generations, handed down by the founder George to his son Richard, and then to Richard's son John. One of its early big contracts was with the Birmingham-Stratford Railway (now the North Warwickshire line). Eminent figures in this firm whom readers may remember include Robert Bloomfield, whose recollections have assisted us in the penning of this article, and a certain very distinguished lawyer who was Deputy Coroner, Clerk of the Peace and President of the Birmingham Law Society and who insisted on being addressed by partners in the time-honoured way, by surname only - Manning Butts.

Shakespeares today, then, has behind it a long tradition of legal

Top left: Tony Jones, right, the current Senior Partner standing with his predecessor Charles Flint. Neil Griffiths of the Monitor Group is seated.
***Below:** With Shakespeares' new Senior Partner Tony Jones (centre) are the six new Partners in 1999 (from left to right) Nicola Walker, Tony Hannington, Paul Meredith, Rohit Deepak, Chris Hill and Lisa Robotham.*

The many foods of Loves

Loves came to Erdington in 1982 in search of bigger premises. Prior to that the catering business had had its home in the village of Stechford, where it had started life as a village greengrocer's in 1913.

Mr Ernest Love, who started the shop, was a firm believer in quality and customer service; he built up a good reputation and traded successfully for many years. By the end of the second world war Ernest was ready to retire. Mr Jack Waldron, who had recently returned from active service, bought the business with his gratuity, and then began looking for ways to expand; a couple of hotels placed orders with him, which he delivered in a black-and-green van, and this was the beginning of Loves' involvement in catering.

Jack Waldron ran the shop until 1961, when he sold it to the Sumner family - Bill and his son Bill. The two Bills opened more shops and began supplying more hotels, and throughout the 60s the business grew. Bill the father retired in the late 60s, and Bill the son took over. Rather than trying to carry on running all the shops and supplying all the catering customers singlehanded, Bill

the son decided to concentrate on the catering, which represented the larger part of the business. All the shops were sold with the exception of the original Stechford shop, which had a lock-up at the back, and Loves' delivery vans - black and yellow by this time - became a regular sight outside the Birmingham hotels. After operating out of the lock-up for several more years Bill moved the business into a new warehouse in Stechford which was far roomier and allowed for future expansion. Bill the father said that Loves would never fill that warehouse, but Bill the son did his best; Loves was becoming market leader in the Midlands, with more and more black and yellow vans delivering more and more different products to more and more catering establishments as Birmingham developed a taste for cosmopolitan cuisine. The more adventurous of the city's chefs were experimenting with new products and new ideas to cater for the increasing number of visitors from overseas, and Loves rose to the challenge, seeking out

Top: *Mr and Mrs Sumner outside their grocers shop in Stechford in the early 1960s.*
Left: *Mr W A Sumner in his shop at 152 Station Road, Stechford.*

exotic fruit and unusual vegetables. All manner of greens began to appear on Birmingham's dinner tables which are now accepted but were then rare, and therefore to be treated with suspicion - things like Iceberg lettuces and avocado pears - and more often than not Loves was the first supplier to put them there.

By 1982 Bill the son had succeeded in filling his warehouse, so he began to look for somewhere even bigger. To make sure that this time they did have enough room to expand, he chose a warehouse four times the size, in Erdington, where Loves still are today - although they have had to add an extra 5,000 square foot of warehousing and install a new 5,000 square foot fridge!

Confusingly, Bill the son was also Bill the father, with his own son Billy, who joined the company around the time of its move to Erdington. These two Bills have continued to keep the area's chefs supplied with a constant flow of new products and new ideas. As the catering industry has expanded, with more and more restaurants opening up and contributing to Birmingham's growing reputation as a good food capital, so Loves has developed into the thriving concern it is today: a progressive plc employing 45 people and serving many of the leading hotels, restaurants and catering establishments throughout the Midlands and beyond. It is also very much a family venture, with a strong 'family' atmosphere among the workforce. Billy took over as Managing Director in 1994 when his father's health showed signs of failing, but Bill, as Chairman, is still very active in the business. A longstanding member of the Midlands Association of Chefs, he was recently made an honorary member in recognition of his service to the industry. His wife Mary, formerly a hairdresser, came to work for the firm shortly after their marriage, and daughter Diane began packing fruit at the age of sixteen; today she is sales

director. Every member of the family shows their loyalty to the business through their commitment to providing the best possible service to every customer, and this has kept Loves at the forefront of the industry. Billy, like his sister, has worked there since he was 16 and has first-hand experience of order picking, driving, accounts, sales, and even sweeping the floor. He firmly believes in investing in the future of the company and the people who work for it - a sure recipe for success!

*Top: The shop on Chester Road, Erdington which became a landmark in the 1980s. Sadly it had to go to make room for the company's expansion and is now offices. **Below:** The Sumner family, clockwise from top left; Mary, Diane, Billy and Bill.*

The most attractive business in Birmingham

At the very beginning of the 20th century, in 1900, the Rapid Magnetting Machine Company Limited was set up by two Birmingham metal trade merchants. This firm initially offered a service to local industries to separate iron from mixed swarf by means of a magnetic extractor; and in 1903 it also began to sell magnetic separators. Herbert Thompson and Arthur Keeling, who were responsible for setting up the business, already had connections with the local metal manufacturers; due to their innovative abilities their venture prospered, and other members of Herbert's family became involved, including Amelia, Horace, and Ernest who was a jeweller by trade. The early separators were made from magnet coils wound from copper wire. One of Rapid's early inventions was a magnetic separator known as the Ore Grader, developed in 1908. The Ore Grader came into its own during the first world war. Armaments were made from special steels, and one of the elements used to produce this hard steel was tungsten. As a result there was a much increased demand for supplies of tungsten, and the Ore Grader was widely used to obtain tungsten from its ores, known as wolframite. These separators are still produced today, and are shipped to countries such as Brazil, Bolivia and Rwanda.

The company subsequently moved from Cambridge Street to Lombard Street, Cheapside, where it was to remain between 1919 and 1975. In 1950 the name of the company was shortened, though not much, to Rapid Magnetic Machines Limited.

Meanwhile one of their employees had left in 1932 to set up on his own; the company he formed was called Electromagnetics, and used the trademark Boxmag. Both Electromagnets and Rapid continued to be run as privately-owned companies, surviving the war and the period of growth which followed. During the late 1950s Electromagnetics had a new factory constructed at Bond Street, on land which it had purchased from King Edward's School. However, in former times

*Top: One of Rapid's early inventions, a magnetic separator known as the Ore Grader, developed in 1908. **Right:** One of the graves disturbed during Electromagnetics' move to their new site at Bond Street in the late 1950s.*

the ground had been a graveyard, and during the course of excavating the foundations for the works a rather unexpected discovery was made: a number of stone coffins were unearthed, which nobody had known were there. These coffins then had to be removed and reconsecrated; fortunately the matter was handled properly, and in the seventeen years that the company remained at those premises there were no reports of ghosts.

In November 1959 Rapid was purchased by Wolseley-Hughes, and less than a decade later, in 1968, Electromagnets followed suit. In 1975 the history of the two companies completed a full circle when they were merged into one. Boxmag Rapid, as it was called, then moved into the premises in Chester Street, Aston, which it still occupies today.

Some of the more complex industrial applications for which magnetic power has been employed over the years seem rather daunting to the non-technical mind, but some, like magnetic floor sweepers to pick up odd screws and bits of wire, and magnets to lift up weighty metal objects, are delightfully simple. A bright little character called Mr Magnaknowhow appeared in Rapid's advertisements during the 1950s and had fun explaining about extracting tramp iron and separating metals.

Having been involved in industrial magnetics since the early days of the industry, Boxmag Rapid has seen, and indeed been responsible for, many advances in technique and applications. Today, magnetic coils are mainly wound from anodised aluminium foil, although copper is still used for certain applications; and many are powered by permanent magnets - including the highest power 'rare earth' magnets. Following a major investment programme, Boxmag Rapid has built a new, more

powerful magnetiser to magnetise 'rare earth' permanent magnets which is larger and stronger than its competitors. The firm's long experience, coupled with its on-going research and development programme, means that it has the ability to engineer equipment to suit a customer's specific requirements - it can, for instance, plastic injection mould, and magnetise complex shapes - in various sectors of UK industry, from food processing to crane manufacturing, reclamation, steel and steel distribution and engineering contractors. Customers abroad are drawn from the same sectors, with additional markets in the mining industry; principal export destinations include Brazil, Iran, Japan, India, Thailand and Malaysia.

Throughout the century the company has continued to explore ways in which its own particular branch of science can benefit industry and the environment, identifying new applications and developing innovative

products to meet them. It has recently been granted patents for separators to clean up the water used in steel-works, and to reclaim waste mortar. So innovation and investment continue at Chester Street, building upon a hundred years of achievement and success. As the new millennium and the firm's centenary approach, Boxmag has a lot to celebrate.

*Top: Staff 'hanging around' for a publicity shoot during the 1950s. **Below left:** The current premises. **Below:** An interior view of the current premises.*

Actions have spoken louder than words for 100 years at BID

Like that of any major city, Birmingham's population has always included a number of deprived people. Fortunately it has also had citizens who have been prepared to offer support to these individuals. In the second half of the 19th century the Birmingham Town Mission, run by a committee of eminent local men, did much charitable work in the city. Prior to 1872 the Mission's principal aim seems to have been to 'alleviate the sufferings of the poor and others in extreme distress' by providing 'shelter, board and clothing'. However, during 1872 the Town Mission set itself two new objectives: to provide a Mission for local cabmen, and religious instruction for the 'deaf and dumb'. The former objective was accomplished by the opening of a Cabmen's Rest in Ratcliffe Place, and the latter by the appointment of a Missioner, Mr W A Griffiths of Alfred Street, to serve the deaf community.

Mr Griffiths was himself one of at least 80 profoundly deaf inhabitants of the city, there were thought to be another 30 living in the Black Country. His work revolved around giving religious services and lectures to groups who met in the school rooms at Graham Street, and visiting the deaf people in their homes, all with a view to their spiritual enlightenment. The great value of his work was recognised; in 1873 subscriptions were invited specifically for the use of the 'Mission to the Deaf and Dumb', and there was talk of raising funds to provide deaf people with a much-needed Mission Hall of their own. Mr Griffiths, assisted by a number of young men who could use sign language, was

devoted to the cause. The Birmingham and Midland Adult Deaf and Dumb Association (founded in 1899 as the Institute for Adult Deaf and Dumb in Birmingham) took over from the Town Mission in 1906, employing Mr Griffiths as missioner. They provided premises in which to hold meetings first at the Police Institute in James Watt Street and then in the former Bible Hall at 316 Broad Street.

Mr Griffiths retired from the work in 1917, partly because of the growing trend towards oral teaching instead of the

Below: *Christmas pantomime at Granville Street Deaf Club 1933.* **Bottom:** *Annual party for deaf people and their families at the Friends Institute, Moseley Road, 1949 (admission was 3 shillings).*

finger-spelling and signing which had always been his own preferred methods of communication. The good work of the Institute continued, broadening its focus over the years from the purely spiritual to the more practical aspects. Finally, in 1932, sufficient funds had been raised to convert a warehouse and stables in Granville Street into a centre for deaf people; this was named the Birmingham Institute for the Deaf and Dumb. Two decades later Birmingham Institute for the Deaf (the word 'dumb' having by this time been dropped from the name) became the first voluntary charity in the UK to be officially responsible for provision of the welfare services which the local authority was legally required to provide for the deaf community, under the 1948 National Assistance Act.

Under the guidance of Eric Ashton, who led the organisation for over 30 years, the work of the Institute, including the development of the Birmingham Deaf Sports and Social Club (BDSSC) established to provide sporting and social facilities for the deaf community, continued to grow. By the early 1970s the Granville Street centre became overcrowded, a building appeal was launched to raise £57,000 and the Institute moved to its present premises in Ladywood Road.

The pioneering work has continued and in 1984 BID began working with the BBC Midlands Today team at Pebble Mill to produce their first news bulletin with sign language which

was shown on BBC2. In 1985 it established the first of two residential homes. Wye Cliff was the first locally run rehabilitation unit for deaf people in the country, set up in partnership with Midland Area Housing Association. In recent years an emphasis has been placed on supporting deaf people to take up their rightful place within the community. BID's initiatives in this sphere have included the implementation of an Employment Service in 1988 to help deaf people find employment, and a scheme launched in 1994 to train deaf people as tutors of sign language at Adult Education Centres. An interpreting unit was established in 1994, a new Deaf Care domiciliary service was pioneered in 1993, and in 1997 Lottery funding made it possible to launch an Information Service and Newspaper, 'Sign Times'.

BID celebrates its centenary in 1999, and it is hoping to mark the occasion with the provision of 12 video telephones, to be located in libraries across the Birmingham and Solihull areas. The videophone, which is far more effective than a textphone, uses the latest technology to enhance communication for deaf people, giving them an unprecedented level of independence through enabling them to communicate in their own language - British Sign Language. Provided BID's appeal raises sufficient funds this centenary project will change communication for deaf people on a scale that is hard for the non-deaf community to imagine. This will rank among BID's many great achievements over its 100 years of service to deaf people in the West Midlands.

Above left: *Older deaf people enjoying their regular get-together at the Deaf Centre in Ladywood Road.* ***Top:*** *The Centre for Deaf People, shortly after its opening in 1973.* ***Right:*** *Today's Videophone - which opens up a new world.*

On the conveyor belt to success

In 1878 Mr George Lane had an opportunity to take over the business in the Digbeth area of Birmingham where he had completed his apprenticeship as a Cabinetmaker two years earlier. He purchased the shop, factory and stock, and started manufacturing occasional furniture and bedding.

By 1892 the company had outgrown the original premises and moved to Brueton Street, Gosta Green, where a four-storey factory, stables and caretaker's house fronting onto Duke Street were acquired. There the company prospered, and George Lane's three sons Harold, Frank and Weston joined the business.

The company manufactured wooden bedsteads, and these needed wire springs. A spring coiling machine was purchased, and in 1897 a patent was taken out for the manufacture of flattened spirals of wire, such as form the basis of all wire conveyor belts; this was used to make foot scrapers which hotels liked to put in their entrance foyers,

but the fashion proved short-lived, and the patent fell into disuse.

George Lane died in 1908, and as part of the work of finalising his estate it was decided to register the company as George Lane & Sons Limited.

The business grew steadily. By 1919 it employed 120 people; in 1921 it bought its first motor lorry for deliveries, and as the stables and caretaker's house were now rendered surplus to requirements they were converted into storage areas and office accommodation. However, by the end of the 1920s the recession was affecting the company. In 1929 the Coventry Chain Company enquired whether they could produce a length of

For continuous feed Furnaces gas or oil fired and for all conveying and mechanical handling.

Above left: *George Lane, founder of the company.*
Above right: *A catalogue of wire conveyor belts pre 1950.* **Below:** *The Brueton Street factory, pre 1940. The lower half of the factory was the old woodworking shop, destroyed by fire in 1940.*

flattened spiral mesh could be produced; someone remembered the patent of 1897, so they accepted the order. The specified length of mesh was duly delivered, and three months later a request came for engineers to go to Coventry and join the two ends together to form a continuous loop. When the engineers returned they reported that the mesh was loaded with components and sent through a red-hot furnace, emerging intact at the other end. In fact, what they had produced was a replacement belt for an American-made state-of-the-art continuous furnace. One former employee still remembers working on that first conveyor belt in 1929; she is in her 90s at the time of writing and has kept in regular contact with the company.

The Conveyor Belt Department grew during the 1930s and accounted for 40 percent of sales in 1939. Unfortunately over the same period the company had suffered more losses than profits. Then in September 1940 an incendiary bomb landed on the factory roof and started a fire which destroyed the woodworking shop and stores. Although it was subsequently rebuilt, this part of the factory was requisitioned by the Ministry of Supplies and at the end of the war the company's rights to it were forfeit. The loss of this area of manufacture put the company in an even worse financial plight, and in 1947 an Extraordinary General Meeting was called to discuss the future. There was no family heir to the business; of George Lane's three sons, Frank was the only survivor, and he was of retirement age. The factory was considered uneconomic for production, and the profit record was poor. All in all, the outlook was bleak, and it was decided to put the company into voluntary liquidation in September 1948.

During the first half of 1947 Frank Lane was taken into hospital for major surgery. Some three months previously, in March 1947, a young engineering graduate had been employed as assistant to the Managing Director. This young man was Ivor Morris. While Frank was in hospital Ivor took over the running of the company; he streamlined the office systems and management, concentrated on the manufacture of wire conveyor belts, and managed to achieve such a spectacular turnaround that the shareholders voted to revoke the decision on voluntary liquidation. Sadly Frank Lane did not live to see this; he died in July 1848.

By the end of 1954 Ivor Morris controlled all of the voting shares of the company. Bedding manufacture continued on a small scale until 1956 when it was decided to withdraw completely from this market and concentrate on the production of wire conveyor belts.

The lease on the Brueton Street factory was due to expire in 1967, and the area was earmarked for redevelopment by the University of Aston. The lease was extended temporarily, and in 1976 the company relocated to a purpose-built factory of 12,750 square feet, with adequate room for expansion, in Garretts Green.

Ivor Morris retired in 1987, and was succeeded as Managing Director by his son John. With an international customer list and strong financial and technical bases, the company enters the 21st century in a strong phase of growth.

Above: *A catalogue of upholstered furniture pre 1940.*
Below: *The premises today.*

The property consultants who get results

Chesterton has contributed to the fortunes of many a Birmingham business, whether by finding the ideal premises for a new venture, or by helping an established company develop a corporate estate strategy, or through one of the many other agency and consultancy services which it offers. Known as Colliers Bigwood Bewlay up to its merger with Chesterton in 1998, the firm has occupied 84 Colmore Row since June 1975, and in fact some 80 years previously the same firm, known then as Edwards, Son & Bigwood, had spent a dozen years in Colmore Row between 1898 and 1910, when it had offices at numbers 17 to 19.

The property firm of Chesterton was founded in 1805. Today, it operates as part of Chesterton International plc, a Group with a turnover of £175.9 million, employing some 2,000 staff and acting as holding company for a number of operating businesses which between them specialise in all aspects of property advice, including selling, letting, valuation, management, facilities management, town planning, development and economic consultancy. All this may seem far removed from the firm's original activities, and it is true that the world of property has advanced a great deal in the century since auctioneers Edwards, Son & Bigwood first came to Colmore Row; but the growth of the firm can be traced from its origins in the mid-19th century to the present day through a succession of

Top centre: An early auction held by Edwards, son & Bigwood.
Right: A brochure for Golden End House, auctioned by the company in 1967.

associations and mergers, each bringing new resources and new expertise.

The firm that was to become Edwards, Son & Bigwood was founded by Mr Henry Edwards. It is known that in 1845 Henry Edwards was trading as a builder from 155 Francis Street, Ashted, and that part of his income came from the collection of rents; he was, then, the company's first property management specialist. He subsequently took his son Samuel into partnership with him. Samuel was born on 26th November 1836 at Duddeston, and was educated at King Edward's Grammar School in New Street, where he showed great promise; it is said that his French master predicted that the boy would one day become Lord Mayor of Birmingham. After leaving school, probably in 1852, he joined his father's business, which was by that time described as a house and estate agent. On May 26th 1869 Edwards & Son relocated to 1 Temple Street, Birmingham, and the firm broadenend its activities to include acting as auctioneer. Samuel went on to become a prominent local figure, thus fulfilling his early promise; a Sunday School superintendent at the age of 17, he went on to become a

non-conformist lay worker, preacher and teacher, associated first with Saltley Congregational Chapel and then with the Steelhouse Lane Ebenezer Chapel. He was respected as an educationalist and a lecturer, held many important chairmanships in public life, particularly in the educational sphere, and served as a Magistrate. He became a member of the Town Council in 1874 and served as Councillor for nine years, being elected Alderman in 1883; he was then elected the first Lord Mayor of Birmingham on 9th November 1900, thus fulfilling his teacher's prediction. He also found time to build the firm of Edwards & Son into one of the most important and successful in the town. By the time of his death in 1920 countless properties, including some very superior residences, had passed through the firm's hands; and Samuel had taken into partnership his son Walter Samuel, and a Mr Ernest James Bigwood.

Although the name of Edwards was retained for many years, the family connection came to an end with Walter Samuel Edwards' death. The Bigwood family connection, however, continued through to modern times. Other families who have played a significant role in the development of the firm are

> *Samuel Edwards built the firm into one of the most important and successful in the town*

too numerous to mention individually, but include the Mathews family, whose practice was taken over in 1938 and who remained in partnership until 1955. An important association with Bewlay Moore & Company of Newhall Street was formed in 1968. Throughout, the firm maintained an active presence in Birmingham, offering an increasing range of services from offices at 158 Edmund Street which it occupied from 1910. It gradually extended its operations to Banbury, Shipston, Stratford-upon-Avon, Tiddington and Oxford, and the firm has been established in London since 1970. An international presence was established in 1981 when an association was formed with Colliers, who had practices in Australia, Hong Kong and Malaysia, and a new office was set up in Washington in that year. The uniting of Colliers Bigwood Bewlay with Chesterton in 1988 has created an organisation which after an illustrious history has now reached the very top of its profession with unparalleled experience, in-depth knowledge, established strengths and resources.

Top: The former Flowers Brewery in Stratford-upon-Avon, one of the many commercial properties sold by Edwards, Bigwood & Bewlay.

Getting a handle on restoration

It would probably not have been in 14 year old Harold McGrail's wildest dreams as he collected spilt coal in a small pony driven cart in a South Wales Colliery that he would eventually become the head of a prestigious brass founders in Birmingham, Armac Manufacturing. The first move in that direction took him to the city to a brass founders in Aston, Barker's, and from there he moved to Ashby's in Buckingham Street who produced cabinet hardware. It was not long, however, before Ashby's had severe financial problems but a 'moonlight flit' to Pullen's Brass Foundry in Moland Street kept the firm alive. Harold soon became manager and in 1931, when the proprietor died, with the help of Mr G Warshaw, a major customer, he took over the firm in partnership with Thomas Armstrong. Thus came the name of the company, ARMAC. The partnership was short-lived, however, and within one year Harold, with his younger brother, Tom, and sister, Eileen, had his own brass foundry, manufacturing cabinet hardware, still in Moland Street. A long way from pony and cart in Wales. The beginnings of the firm coincided with the depression which was sweeping the industrial world and times were hard. The staff were paid piecemeal with whatever money could be gleaned from customers.

The war proved to be somewhat of a saviour for, despite losing many employees to the services and to the vital Spitfire assembly plant in Castle Bromwich, Armac managed to be registered for war work, producing portholes for ships and components for radar equipment. In the 1950s there was a rationing of brass for manufacture as the country tried to recover from the debilitating effects of the war. As the economy of the country began to recover during the next decade, the company began to prosper. It left the original premises in Moland Street in 1958 to move to the present one, just round the corner in Staniforth Street. In those days it was a very labour intensive factory, running belt-driven polishing and turning lathes, working exclusively in brass sand castings.

Above left: *Harold McGrail, founder of the company.*
Below: *The premises in the 1970s with Armac's present building, to the left, under construction.*

It suffered a serious setback in 1980 as result of a fire which led to a major disruption in production, as the factory had to be rebuilt. At the same time the early 1980s meant another recession and the firm had now two battles to fight. Battle it did only to come face to face, as was the case with much of the traditional manufacturing industry, with another far worse economic recession in the early 1990s.

The family tradition throughout the years has been maintained, firstly in 1960 when Harold's son, Bryan, joined the firm, assuming control in 1980 when Harold retired. Bryan is now the Chairman and his three sons have taken control of what is now the Armac Group of five companies in the Birmingham area, each involved in various aspects of the brassfoundry business.

Now it is a very modern plant with large CNC machines and automatic finishing equipment working in a multitude of brass components from several sources of supply. Emphasis is now on hot brass forgings, pressure die-castings, turned parts, pressed work and still the traditional sand castings. The company's main markets are in the reproduction furniture industry and antique restoration trade. Armac's reputation for high quality products, authenticity of design and the variety and size of range of its products available has made its name widely known throughout this country and abroad. That is its simple business philosophy and furniture makers the world over are very much aware of this. They recognise and appreciate a much superior

product than Armac's rivals', especially in the meticulous finishing techniques applied to all the firm's products. The main battle is a familiar one - against inferior imports and cheaper alternative materials. Armac will continue to strive for quality against this, consolidating its own position in the home market and extending its high profile in the export trade. The company has one obvious aim and that is for furniture makers all over the world to be able to make use of its products and recognise their source.

Very small beginnings indeed from a pit in Wales to a desperate situation in 1931 and then to a high profile company. And yet what would have happened if there had not been a St John Ambulance man on the staff in 1947? Harold McGrail had a fondness for salt on his food and that nearly had fatal consequences. One lunchtime Eileen, his sister, an employee called Dodd and Harold each had a ham sandwich and each sprinkled it with what they thought was salt but which was in fact caustic soda crystals kept in a domestic container. Soon each was sick and suffered violent stomach pains. Quick action was needed and that saved their lives. That member of staff recognised what had occurred and all were rushed to hospital. The three were saved and so was the firm. The consequences could have been disastrous for both family and firm. Good fortune and quick thinking saved the day.

Above: *The premises today.*

Sapcote - Building on good foundations

William Sapcote served his seven years apprenticeship in Market Harborough after which, in 1832, he walked to Birmingham, working as a freelance 'journeyman' (qualified) carpenter as he went. Twenty one years later he bought his master's business for £73-6s-10d (£73.34p) in the year that Britain declared war on Russia. He made steady progress employing 18 men and boys for a total of £15 per six day week. By the 1870s Sapcotes were doing work for Lloyd's Bank to be followed twenty years after with contracts for public libraries and the M&B Brewery. In between he built the beautiful red brick Gothic styled Birmingham School of Art, now a deservedly listed building, within the agreed price of £20,000.

The Edwardian era saw Sapcotes build the handsome Lloyd's Bank on Colmore Row and a few years later more Lloyd's branches in Harbourne, Caernarvon and Temple Row. Other stylish modern buildings included several Science blocks for King Edward's Grammar School and the Hill Street Telephone Exchange, of 1907, showed that Sapcotes were chosen by those at the 'leading edge' of contemporary technology. The important Gold Assay Office in the Jewellery Quarter selected this go ahead family firm to build its new premises.

Left: Mr William Sapcote who bought the company from a Mr Brighton in 1853. *Below:* Sapcote builders working on the old MEB power station in Summer Lane in 1925. *Bottom:* The Sapcote premises on Camden Street.

Cadburys, only a year older than Sapcotes, ordered the company Gym and 'Q' Block from the well established Birmingham builders, which went on to build stables at the Harbourne Institution of the Blind followed by more work for M&B Brewery. The outbreak of war in 1914 brought no slackening of trade as contracts were completed on libraries and hospitals, banks and insurance offices. War or no war life must go on.

The years immediately after the 1918 Armistice were marked by a generous national outpouring of funds, quite out of proportion to the communities which donated them, for the erection of war memorials including that in Wolverhampton, erected by Sapcote.

In spite of the enervating effects of the Great Depression the inter-war years saw Sapcotes involved in projects on Northfield, Aston and Stratford-upon-Avon parish churches plus public sporting and bathing facilities. The firm was also employed by Birmingham Children's Hospital and two well known local schools, namely the Edgbaston Preparatory School (Hallfield) and Edgbaston Church of England College for Girls.

The harshly rationed war years of the 1940s saw Sapcotes involved in essential war work such as building Air Raid Shelters, camouflaging the Cadbury's Factory at Bournville and repairing war damaged facilities for the London Midland and Scottish Railway Company. Immediate post war clients included Birmingham University, the Dental Hospital, the historic Gardens of the Birmingham Botanical Society and Shrieve's House in Stratford-upon-Avon. The latter was followed by work, in 1950, on Mary Arden's House, Wilmcote, the lovely home of Shakespeare's mother. After this restoration project the Trustees of the Lord Leycester Hospital for Old Soldiers hired Sapcotes for similar work. Later the Shakespeare Trust returned to Sapcotes for work on the better known cottage of the Bard's love, Anne Hathaway.

By way of contrast Sapcotes in the Swinging Sixties again took on work for Birmingham University, refurbished the Post and Mail building in New Street, a chain of Midland railway stations and Birmingham Cathedral (the former Parish Church in Colmore Row) and converted a redundant chemical works into small industrial units. The latter was a sign of the times, to be repeated in Aston and West Bromwich, as larger, well established works gave way to small businesses of the ilk that made early Birmingham famous as the 'workshop of the world'. The severely beautiful Town Hall, beloved of generations of concert goers, also received the Sapcote treatment of careful craftsmanship and scholarly adherence to original plans and designs during restoration.

And so the Sapcote Story continues, a rich medley of prestigious restoration projects, to show visitors from home and abroad that the family's tradition of high class craftsmanship is as strong as ever, married with cost effective work to the same standards for the industrial and commercial clients upon whom depends the wealth of the Midlands. Competitors, great and small, come and go but the Sapcote reputation, dependant on firm leadership and a skilled team, remains true in a family business alive to the modern market.

Top: The Company offices in 1937 and a Bedford truck in the firm's livery of cream with brown lettering. The driver is Stan Wright who completed over 30 years as driver and yard foreman.
Below: Sapcote restored Anne Hathaway's Cottage in 1969 when it was nearly destroyed by fire.

On target for the 21st century

widely regarded as the best in Europe; equipped with machinery made to the company's own design, it was capable of producing a perfectly-finished bore to extremely fine tolerances. Since becoming part of the UK engineering group Modular Industries the firm has benefited from hi-tech engineering facilities which perfectly complement the more traditional and established skills needed for precision gun-making. Parker-Hale now looks forward to a 21st century in which Birmingham's long-established gun-making industry, now enjoying unprecedented levels of advanced development and technological opportunities, will continue to provide an excellent range of equipment to military establishments and shooting sportsmen all over the world.

Parker-Hale's catalogues today offer a wide range of specialist weapons, quality firearms and shooting accessories for the international market. This represents a significant diversification in product in the 120 years or so since the firm began, but one thing that has remained constant is the engineering precision with which every item is made.

Mr A G Parker, the founder, was a rifleman with the 1st Battalion, the Royal Warwickshire Regiment, and he first began manufacturing gun barrels, rifles and accessories in 1880, although he did not officially establish a business until 1890. His nephew Mr A T C Hale, also a keen rifleman, joined him as a partner in 1900, and it was Mr Hale who invented the Parkerifling system of re-barrelling, which was used to convert service rifles to .22" calibre for use in training new recruits in 1914. During its early years the firm also made a range of precision rifle sights and various cleaning accessories including the famous Youngs .303 Rifle Oil. Mr Parker died in 1915 and the company passed first to Mr Hale, who was released from the army so that the firm could continue its valuable war work. Assisted by the sons of the two families, Mr A C T Hale remained at the head of the firm until his death in 1952. The name was changed to Parker-Hale Limited in 1936.

Among the many excellent products which have helped establish Parker-Hale's reputation over the years are its 7.62mm cal. Sniper Rifle which many governments adopted for military use, its unsurpassed range of shotguns, and its range of reproduction rifles which are re-creations of famous historic pieces such as the .577 Enfield Minie Rifle which was used during the American Civil War. After its move to Golden Hillock Road in 1963 Parker-Hale set up a barrel producing plant which is still

Top left: The hydraulic copying lathe, pictured in the mid 1960s. ***Above:*** *A photograph advertising telescopic sights from a late 1960s cataglogue.* ***Below:*** *A selection of modern-day rifle scopes.*

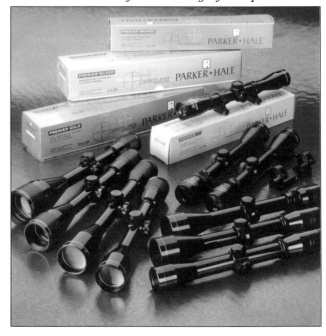

'Henley' brand bakeware

'Brummagen ware' in all its many aspects is world famous and no less so in the popular baking dishes made by Dunnetts of Birmingham. This family firm was founded in 1885 by Mr Rivers Dunnett who traded as a Manufacturing Ironmonger in Bristol Street. In those days cooks had little choice but to man-handle hefty cast iron pots and pans around the equally black cast iron ranges. Cottagers in rural areas still cooked on open fires using small size witches' cauldrons and three legged pots for family cooking in a fashion that demanded sturdy construction.

run kitchens to fit in with a lifestyle which included work and/or a busy social life. Heavy, rust collecting utensils did not figure at all in her desires which were catered for by Dunnetts who provided all that was modern, light and easy to clean for the proud cook of the all-electric kitchen. During those decades housewives were proud of their home baking and the splendid teas that featured on the tables of middle class and artisan homes alike.

Early in the 1900s his sons, Howard and Hanbury, took charge as equal partners naming the firm Dunnett Brothers and moving, first to Angelina Street and then Loveday Street before settling in the present premises in King's Road, Tyseley in 1922. Four years later the partnership was dissolved leaving Hanbury Dunnett in charge, trading under the name Dunnetts.

It was the introduction of gas and electric cookers in the interwar years that led to the development of lighter weight, tin plated steel oven-ware, a movement hastened by servantless ladies entering unfamiliar kitchen quarters and finding them wanting. The housewife of the 30's, 40's and 50's, let alone the 90's, wanted easy to

'300 RANGE'
Non-Stick Bakeware
WITH NEW TEFLON 2

SANDWICH PANS

	Size in inches	Size in cms
No. 351/7	7 dia. x 1 deep	17.5 dia. x 2.5 deep
No. 351/8	8 dia. x 1 deep	20.0 dia. x 2.5 deep
PACK 12		

ROUND CAKE PANS

	Size in inches	Size in cms
No. 352/7	7 dia. x 2 deep	17.5 dia. x 5.0 deep
No. 352/8	8 dia. x 2½ deep	20.0 dia. x 5.6 deep
No. 352/9	9 dia. x 2½ deep	22.5 dia. x 6.3 deep
PACK 12		

12-HOLE BUN TRAYS

	Size in inches	Size in cms
No. 353 Domed Cups	12 x 9½	30.0 x 23.8
No. 354 Tapered Cups	12 x 9½	30.0 x 23.8
PACK 12		

9-HOLE BUN TRAYS

	Size in inches	Size in cms
No. 356 Domed Cups	9½ x 9½	23.8 x 23.8
No. 357 Tapered Cups	9½ x 9½	23.8 x 23.8
PACK 12		

"Henley" — quality bakeware with longer lasting Teflon 2 coating. Available in

The war years saw Dunnetts making bomb fins and Land Army boxes for the Ministry of Supply. Since those rationed days Dunnetts, now managed by Geoffrey and his sister Mrs Cressey, have returned to providing for the cooking housewife who buys her baking and roasting tins, pans and trays at the supermarket and who expects reliability at a fair price.

Top left (square picture): *Rivers Dunnett, founder of the company.* ***Top left (oval picture):*** *Hanbury Dunnett, the founder's son.*
Top right: *George and William Dunnett.*
Above centre: *A page from the company's catalogue of 1979.*

The firm whose products are bound to please the customer

Kelly's Directory of 1856 includes the following entry: 'Mills, Henry - printer and page numberer 4 King Edward's Place'. Mr Henry Mills, the inventor and manufacturer of machines for the numerical printing of Cloakroom tickets, had set up in business at this address just off Broad Street the previous year; he later passed on his business to his two nephews Frederick and William Mills. The activities of the firm expanded, and in 1899 moved to 56-60 Cornwall Street, where expansion continued. It was at this stage that William Francis Lawrence was appointed Works Manager, beginning a family connection which is today in its third and fourth generation.

William Lawrence was born in Somerset, and ran away at the age of 14 to Bristol with the intention of going to sea. He was caught on the dockyard and instead became apprenticed to a Bristol bookbinder. He then moved to Birmingham and got a job with Davis & Company, where he rose to the position of foreman bookbinder. In 1889 he married Alice Elford, an employee of the Bristol firm. William and Alice had two sons, Alfred William (killed in action in the first world war) and Bernard Caswell.

In 1914 William Lawrence decided that he could do better with a company of his own, but was persuaded to make a management buy-out of Henry Mills, forming a Limited Liability Company with himself as Managing Director at the princely sum of "three pounds and five shillings payable weekly".

On his death in 1925 B C Lawrence took over, continuing until 1956 as Managing Director when his son, Philip William Lawrence, succeeded him. The current Managing Director, Andrew Philip Lawrence (Philip's son) took over in 1998.

Over the years Henry Mills Limited has overcome a number of challenges, including the destruction of its premises in Cornwall Street in 1940, economic recessions and a major burglary in 1994, and it has continued to move with the times. A delivery and collection service started in 1927 when the firm acquired a Morris van, and the range of

processes carried out over the years includes showcard mounting, label punching, loose leaf piercing, plastabbing (affixing plastic tabs onto card), film laminating, Stencil gluing and Wiro binding. Equipment has been constantly updated as better machines became available - from a 1938 Cundall folding machine, through the Macey-gather-stitch-trim-line installed in 1973, to major investment in 1980 in a new Macey gather-stitcher, Sulby perfect binder, B1 and SRA1 folding machines and pharmaceutical folder, and, more recently still, Scott Ten Thousand plastabbing machines, a Busch Ram punching machine and a Setmaster 24 station collating machine.

The company moved to its current premises in Chester Street in 1978. Offering virtually every imaginable bookbinding and print finishing process except printing, Henry Mills prides itself on its well-earned reputation for quality and reliability...and you can count on a firm which has been in the numbering business for more than 140 years!

Top left: *William Francis Lawrence, left - the first generation of the Lawrences to work at Henry Mills with his son Bernard Caswell Lawrence in 1916.* **Left:** *A Henry Mills staff Christmas Dinner, 1935. BC Lawrence is in the centre of the top table, wearing a bow tie.* **Above:** *The Shadwell Street premises occupied by Henry Mills from 1945 to 1977.*

The firm that makes the most of its clients' ideas

Intellectual property rights - patents, copyright, trademarks, designs and suchlike - can, as many people have found to their cost, be a minefield where mistakes are expensive. Certainly it is an area where there is no substitute for expertise and experience. Barker Brettell, which has specialised in intellectual property protection for well over a century, has both.

Its origins probably date back to around 1850, but the present firm began as George Barker in 1875. Mr Barker, formerly a consultant engineer, was joined by Mr F G Brettell in 1891, and from offices at 75/77 Colmore Row, Birmingham, the two chartered patent attorneys dealt with patents, copyright, designs and trademarks, the latter being Mr Brettell's particular speciality.

In 1928 Mr W O Duncan joined, and the firm changed its name to Barker, Brettell and Duncan. Each of the three founder members served as President of the Chartered Institute of Patent Agents, and the family connections were carried into the next generation with the involvement of W O Duncan's son (Mr A H Duncan - another President of the CIPA), George Barker's nephew, and Mr Brettell's son-in-law. The firm has continued to thrive with a very loyal, willing and able workforce including many long-serving members of staff.

Barker, Brettell and Duncan remained in Colmore Row until 1957, with the exception of a spell during the second world war when they had to move out of the city centre and work from Mr Brettell's home - combining this with air raid warden duties. They then moved to 16 Greenfield Crescent, Edgbaston, and in 1974 the firm moved to its current premises at 138 Hagley Road, which are at the time of writing undergoing extensive renovation.

Renamed Barker Brettell in 1998, this highly-respected practice provides a first class professional service to all levels of client, from the giant multi-national corporation to private individual. The Midlands-based mechanical and engineering companies that formed the traditional client base have now been joined by chemical, electrical, electronic, computer and biotechnology companies, and the firm's overseas activities are growing year by year. Barker Brettell's resources are extensive and the firm is always ready to take on new challenges. Whatever the sphere of activity, clients can rely on Barker Brettell's decisive thinking and expert advice; and the firm's policy of clear language, rather than confusing legal jargon, is also greatly appreciated by clients.

Top left: George Barker, the firm's founder.
Above: The firm's headquarters in Edgbaston.
Below: Christopher Spall, current Senior Partner of the firm. Chris is a mechanical engineer who is also a specialist in the patent matters of the firm's principal automotive and electrical engineering clients, both local and overseas.

These were among the thousands of Birmingham schoolchildren who were evacuated to escape German bombing in the early stages of World War II.

Acknowledgments

The photographs appearing on the following pages are courtesy of Birmingham Library Services:
Title page, 3, 4, 5, 6, 7, 8, 9, 10, 11, 12, 13, 14, 15, 16, 17, 18, 19, 20, 21, 22, 23, 24, 25, 26, 27, 28, 29, 30, 31, 32, 33, 34, 35, 36, 37, 38, 39, 40, 41, 48, 49, 50, 51, 52, 53, 61, 62, 63, 64, 65, 66, 132

Thanks are also due to:
Margaret Thompson
Women's Royal Voluntary Services - South West Division
Peter Thomas who penned the editorial text
and Margaret Wakefield and Mike Kirke for their copywriting skills